Books by Guy Davenport

EVERY FORCE
EVOLVES A FORM

Twenty Essays by

GUY DAVENPORT

North Point Press
San Francisco

The author and publisher are grateful for permission to reproduce the following: *The Happy Quartet (Adam and
Eve)* by Henri Rousseau, from the Collection of Mrs. John
Hay Whitney; *Merry Jesters (Joyeux Farceurs)* by Henri
Rousseau, oil on canvas, 57 ½ × 44 ¾ inches, 1906, Philadelphia Museum of Art: The Louise and Walter Arensberg
Collection; *Portrait of Pierre Loti* by Henri Rousseau, oil on
canvas, 61 cm by 50 cm, 1910, collection of Kunsthaus Zü-
rich; *The Street* by Balthus, oil on canvas, 6′ 4 ¾″ × 7′ 10 ½″,
1933, collection, The Museum of Modern Art, New York,
James Thrall Soby Bequest.

North Point Press
850 Talbot Avenue
Berkeley, California
94706

For Rodney Needham

[The Celtic smith who cut the die for this silver coin was trying to make iconographic sense of others derived from a stater of Philip II of Macedonia, which bore
a head of Hermes on one side and a winged horse on the other. Copy after copy,
over centuries, provincial mints in Aquitania had already misread the face of
Hermes as a lion's head, as sun and moon, or as so many abstract lines and dots.
Here Hermes' profile has become the head and forelegs of a horse, his hair and
neck its rump and wing. Horse has been an Aquitanian sign from Lascaux to the
midyear centaurs who still dance as what the English call the Hobby Horse, on out
to the bull ring horses of Goya (drawn in Bordeaux), the quagga-mounted utopian
hordes of Fourier, and the St.-Simoniste horses of Rosa Bonheur. All art is a dance
of meaning from form to form].

Contents

Foreword

I fancy mankind may come, in time, to write all
aphoristically, except in narrative; grow weary
of preparation, and connection, and illustration,
and all those arts by which a big book is made.
                                    SAMUEL JOHNSON
              (in Boswell's *The Journal of a Tour of the Hebrides*)

My title, which sounds like Heraclitus or Darwin, is from Mother Ann Lee
(1736–1784), founder of the Shakers. In its practical sense, this axiom was
the rule by which Shaker architects and designers found perfect forms. The
American broom is a Shaker invention: a flat brush of sedge stems, sturdily
bound, and with a long handle. Previously the broom, such as Parisian street-
cleaners still use, was a fascicle of twigs, which one stoops to use. The Shaker
broom *sweeps*. One's upright stance in using it has dignity. It is a broom that
means business. We are told that Mother Ann, overseeing the high art of
sweeping Shaker rooms (the first uncluttered, clear interior domestic space
in a century of china-shop impediments) would shout, "There is no dirt in
heaven!"

    As an ideal, that form is the best response to the forces calling it into being
has been the genius of good design in our time, as witness Gropius, Le Cor-
busier, Rietveldt, Mondriaan, Sheeler, Fuller. A work of art is a form that
articulates forces, making them intelligible. These studies, most of which
were written for editors, are all, one way or another, considerations of ideas

and their realization, instigations, innovations, renovations; that is, of force and form.

"The Champollion of Table Manners," "Imaginary Americas," "Making It Uglier to the Airport," and "In That Awful Civil War" were first published in *The Hudson Review*; "Balthus" and "What Are Those Monkeys Doing?" (under the title "Rousseau"), in *Antaeus*; "Transcendental Satyr" (under the title "Satyr and Transcendentalist"), in *Parnassus*; "The Smith of Smiths," "More Genteel than God," and "The Peales and Their Museum," in *Inquiry*. "Montaigne" is reprinted from *Montaigne's Travel Journal*, translated by Donald M. Frame (North Point Press, 1983), "Herondas" from *The Mimes of Herondas*, my translation (Grey Fox Press, 1981), and "Nabokov's Don Quixote" from *The New York Times Book Review* and Vladimir Nabokov, *Lectures on Don Quixote*, edited by Fredson Bowers (Harcourt Brace Jovanovich, 1983). "Late Beckett" appeared in the *Washington Post Book World*, "Pergolesi's Dog" in the *New York Times*. "The Artist as Critic," "The Scholar as Critic," and "The Critic as Artist" (a filched title) were read at Washington and Lee University as the Arthur and Margaret Glasgow Lectures for 1985 and published in *Shenandoah*. "Ariadne's Dancing Floor" was written for a collection of essays on Joyce that failed to materialize. "Every Force Evolves a Form" is an unabashedly experimental inclusion: it is simply a lecture, reconstructed from notes on a scrap of paper, for English 684 at the University of Kentucky. It was, like all my classroom lectures, invented on my half an hour's daily walk to work. As all my ideas, such as they are, come from these walks, and from the classrooms at the end of them, it will perhaps interest a reader or two to see the raw matter of a class.

EVERY FORCE
EVOLVES A FORM

The Champollion
of Table Manners

Table manners, we learn in Claude Lévi-Strauss' ungivingly tedious book *The Origin of Table Manners*,[1] are one of our subtlest lines separating civility from barbarity, an orderly barrier erected against chaos, and a set of gestured signals that began when the first two people to share a brained tapir trusted each other enough to eat together. Ungivingly tedious: the book is laughably mistitled. It is an analysis of several hundred Amazonian and Plains Indian myths, as well as a continuation of the elaborate structuralist theory of culture which began two volumes back with *The Raw and the Cooked* and *From Honey to Ashes*. Table manners are first mentioned on page 307. We do not see the phrase again until page 427. Not until page 471 do we leave the rain forest and prairie to hear an intense, brilliant, and brief discourse on what all that has gone before has to do with table manners.

Obliquity is the structuralist trademark. There is always something to be explained before something else can be explained. We begin with many versions of a myth about a clinging woman, "The Hunter Monmanéki and His Wives," from the Tucuna of South America. We don't know it yet, but the essence of the book is all here in this strange and apparently pointless tale. The hero gets a frog pregnant by pointing his penis at her, they marry, go hunting together, and straightway bump into the fact that they dine on wholly different things, and the hunter's mother has a sharp word for a daughter-in-law who serves cockroaches as a delicacy. Our hero marries four more wives, with indifferent success. One of them breaks in half at the

---

[1] Claude Lévi-Strauss, *The Origin of Table Manners: Introduction to a Science of Mythology*: 3, trans. John and Doreen Weightman (New York: Harper and Row, 1978).

waist. When he tries to abandon her, the top half clings to his back and appropriates his food. Indian myths tend to be Bosch-like, nightmarish, strange.

Some fifty transmutations and variants of this myth later, we move to North America to hear another set. These also have to do with marrying frogs. Sun and Moon, looking down on the earth one day, decided to choose wives from the creatures below. Moon chose a maiden, but Sun, who did not like the squint on human faces when they looked at him, chose a frog. The mother of Sun and Moon was willing to be charmed by both her daughters-in-law, though Frog Wife came under suspicion immediately, because she peed at every hop. The test, however, was table manners. The wedding feast was a nice mess of buffalo chitterlings. The Indian wife crunched hers with a fine loud smacking noise and was much admired. Poor Frog Wife did not even know which was the food and which the fire beneath. She fished out a piece of charcoal, sucked on it, and let black spit run down her chin. This made everybody sick. Moon was derisive. Frog Wife jumped on his face and stayed there, like the clinging woman in the South American myth.

These tales, told over thousands of years around the campfire, display upon careful inspection and comparison something like a genetic code programmed with all the anxieties and intuition that have fed into it generation after generation. The myth of the clinging woman, for instance, contains a submerged pattern that has to do with the fishing seasons and the constellations that signal their beginning and end. It encodes a creation myth about the stars known as "Berenice's Hair." The twist of its plot is a message about marrying too close (incest) and too far off (incompatible *mores*). The ultimate structure that serves as an armature is the Indian feeling for periodicity, measure, a just balance to things.

Once upon a time Sun and Moon were brothers who were always together in the sky. Hence there was no night, no seasons. Things cosmic had to be separated out so that events occurred at regular intervals. Nine months for a pregnancy, menstruation every month, the rainy season immediately following the rising of a constellation: a measured beat to time was, to the Indian imagination, an heroic victory after a struggle among diverse wills.

All four volumes of *An Introduction to a Science of Mythology* are orchestrations rather than simple melodies (the analogy to music is Lévi-Strauss'). The largest scheme is a breakthrough into the culture that may be the oldest we are ever likely to know, the sub-Arctic nomads of the Old Stone Age. They ringed the northern hemisphere right around, and descended to populate the Americas. (Lévi-Strauss thinks that the Indians of North America came from the south, or at least that there have been migrations both ways. A myth involving maple syrup in North America parallels one involving honey in South America.)

Then there is a harmony of transmutations. Sometimes they run along a scale such as from raw to cooked, exquisitely graduated along the line (there is a fine cadenza on the boiled and the roasted at the end of this volume). Sometimes they are transmutations of symbols in the grammar of myth (as in part 6, chapter 2, where Lévi-Strauss decodes an elaborate and wonderfully confusing association in the Plains Indian imagination of quillwork, pubic hair, stones, scalps, dandruff, sun and moon). Essentially we are faced with hieroglyphs throughout this study, with Lévi-Strauss as our Champollion. The message we are reading is always how culture crosses over from nature. That is, how humanity has civilized itself.

Lévi-Strauss compares himself to a geologist: history is stratified. Freud, he points out, was something like a geologist, working with the layers of individual minds. It is well-known by now that Lévi-Strauss is a kind of modern Rousseau and does not like to contrast the primitive and the advanced. Cultures deal with the human condition differently, but these differences are not necessarily degrees of superiority or vitality. We have science to turn to in sickness, a Nambikwara or Nuer has herbs and the witch doctor; and yet what primitive people lose to disease and the marauding tiger we lose to war, traffic, and the killing pace of industrial life.

And why know about the Indian's obsession with the canoe journey of the sun and the moon in the days before time began? Lévi-Strauss keeps seeing a moral. The history of table manners shows that industrial man has subverted their purpose, which was to keep the boorishness of people from contaminating the world. The cookpot and the table are woman's domain; she is close to the world's hard-won cosmic order, as she is a periodic creature. She creates with her body; she is in sympathy with the moon and the seasons. Table manners arise from an intuition that human manners are a contract with the world's order. Ritual acknowledges gods and natural forces.

But all this curious knowledge begins to explain things that our attention might never otherwise have focused on. In Dorothy Sayers' *Gaudy Night*, for instance, Lord Peter Wimsey finally wins the hand of Harriet Vane. She is the daughter of a country doctor. Lord Peter has got her off a murder charge, but she nevertheless has complex reasons for turning down the dashing, clever aristocrat. She changes her mind and admits her own denied love on a picnic in a punt on the Cherwell. At the same time, Lord Peter is surer than ever of his love. For one thing, Harriet knows how to sit properly in a punt, and recognizes Lord Peter's expertise as a punter. Their rustic meal turns out to be delightful, for they are at ease eating with each other. The picnic basket, of course, is between them in the punt.

This romantic rigmarole would make fine sense to an Amazon Indian. The canoe is a symbol of cosmic harmony (or any other kind: either you know how to paddle a canoe, rower at the front, steersman at the back, the family goods in the middle, or you find yourself among the piranhas and alligators). It is, moreover, a transmutation of the family hearth, for a pot of embers is among the household goods in the middle, and proper canoe manners are emblematic of an harmonious marriage. So the Amazonian would say of Dorothy Sayers' saccharine scene, *Ah yes*! They like the same food, they have the same table manners, his mother will not have a fit when she sees her, and she is a woman who knows how to sit properly in a canoe. Her behavior will not jolt the periodicity of the cosmos.

And there are two moments in literature that I have always found appalling. One is in Scott's *The Antiquary*. The old mendicant factotum Edie Ochiltree (compared several times to Diogenes for his simplicity, wisdom, and ironic tongue) has helped everybody in the novel, some to a family fortune, some to success in courtship, some to self-knowledge. And yet when there is a moment for a round of congratulations over food and drink, we have: "A table was quickly covered in the parlour, where the party sat joyously down to some refreshment. At the request of Oldbuck, Edie Ochiltree was permitted to sit by the sideboard in a great leathern chair, which was placed in some measure behind a screen." *Was permitted to sit! Behind a screen!*

The other outrage is in a note of Malone's to Boswell: "Soon after Savage's Life [by Johnson] was published, Mr. Harte dined with Edward Cave, and occasionally praised it. Soon after, meeting him, Cave said, 'You made a man very happy t'other day.'—'How could that be, says Harte; 'nobody was there but ourselves.' Cave answered, by reminding him that a plate of victuals was sent behind a screen, which was to Johnson, dressed so shabbily, that he did not choose to appear; but on hearing the conversation, he was highly delighted with the encomiums on his book."

Here we have an agreement among people dining that an eater be segregated as unseemly. A code of propriety overrides every other consideration. We read in *The Tale of Mrs. Tiggy-Winkle*: "Mrs. Tiggy-Winkle's hand, holding the tea-cup, was very brown, and very, very wrinkly with the soap-suds; and all through her gown and her cap there were *hair-pins* sticking wrong end out; so that Lucie didn't like to sit too near her." Beatrix Potter's illustration shows them sitting at the extreme ends of a bench, like Indians in a canoe, and a saucer sits between them.

Lord knows what anthropological history there is beneath the screening off of Ochiltree and Johnson; Lévi-Strauss would no doubt talk about it in terms of near and far, and give examples of other ways of being far while actually being near.

A social structure is always something we know without knowing that we know. Lévi-Strauss is at his most entertaining when he shows us that we know systems, for instance, of names. We can distinguish a racehorse's name from that of a cat without any sense of how we know this. We *feel* categorical sets. We can all spot a person without proper table manners without being able to specify his sins. Outside our culture we would be at a loss, ignorant of the *bon ton* of the place. A time-machine invitation to dinner with Elizabeth I would unnerve us: She ate with her fingers, and her chair was lower than ours, to diminish the distance between dish and face.

The fork came to the United States from Bordeaux, by way of the diplomatic corps during the Revolution (to Bordeaux from England, to England from Venice); one would like to know who turned it over American and French fashion. The English use it tines down, and pile food on it with a knife. Montaigne on his journey to Italy and the spas (for the stone) had a keen eye for table manners. Individual goblets were just coming in, replacing the common flagon. It is clear that a history of table manners, especially to the structuralist eye, would be a peculiarly telling evolution of man as a social creature.

Aristotle wrote a *Rules for the Mess Table*; it hasn't come down to us. Ptahotep wrote on table manners (2675 B.C.): "If you are at table with someone of greater standing, take only the food you are offered. Don't watch his plate; keep your eyes on yours. Lower your head when spoken to. Speak only when asked. Laugh when the distinguished person laughs, and in such a manner as to please him." Table manners engaged the attention of Plutarch and Erasmus.

"It remains to be seen," Lévi-Strauss writes at the end of this intricate study of primitive civility, "whether man's victory over his powerlessness, when carried to a state out of all proportion to the objectives with which he was satisfied during the previous millennia of his history, will not lead back to unreason." That is, have we moved irrevocably beyond the ethics encoded in archaic myths; and if so, where are we? Sartre's "Hell is other people" is "not so much a philosophical proposition as an ethnographical statement about our civilization."

The primitive mind sees disorder in itself and enlists every discipline to keep from contaminating the world. We, says Lévi-Strauss, see all disorder outside ourselves, in the world and in other people; our anxiety is that they will contaminate us: botch our composure, snatch our opportunities, queer our luck.

When myth exhausts its power to transmit messages (how to marry, how to eat, how to be brave), it becomes a narrative that does not know how to resolve itself. Everything, says the contemporary novel, comes to a bad end. (It was in Victorian times that novels began to have ambiguous, unresolved, ironic endings.) Music, too, refuses to be harmonic. We are no wiser than man has ever been about our helplessness in nature. Our fate with love, death, despair, doubt, wealth, courage, everything that's human, is no different after all those years of yearning for a better context. We've got here (to the electric light, the Buick, antibiotics, TV) bringing along practically everything we accumulated along the way. We still eat, with or without manners. We still dream idiotic and awful images. We still draw, sculpt, enrapture ourselves with music, dance, pray, and keep superstitions that would make a Malay laugh. As there is no absolute definition of a human being, it is unanswerable to ask if we have remained human. We have remained Jewish, Catholic, Sicilian, French, Presbyterian. Before that we were savages terrified of thunder, worshipful of fermented grape juice, wondering whether the gods allow us to marry our sister, first, or second cousin. We still have no information as to how races branched out from each other, where we first lived, where civilization arose. Our past is forgotten. We can forget it again.

Lévi-Strauss comes from two immediate disciplines, the French sociologists Émile Durkheim and his nephew Marcel Mauss, and the British school of anthropology, Tylor, Radcliffe-Brown, Evans-Pritchard, Needham. He is quick to mention his deep debt to American ethnographers and folklorists. He seems to have learned from everybody. His mind is too original to be the exponent of a master or a school. His Marx, Rousseau, and Freud are not anybody else's. He claims to have a Neolithic mind: one that makes a foray, brings down its game, and forgets. His autobiography, *Tristes tropiques* (only last year translated into English in its full text) is a classic in modern French literature because of its presentation of anthropology as an intellectual and personal quest.

He is, to my knowledge, the best and most diligent interpreter of our time. I would like to think that he will be ranked higher than Freud as a reader of riddles and a rediscoverer of the primacy of human behavior in our knowledge of the world. To his distress (or amusement) his discipline has flowed beyond its anthropological and linguistic contours into literary criticism ("another Parisian fad," he remarks) and other endeavors. *Structuralism* has become a rage; structuralist books are kept locked behind glass in the bookstores around the Sorbonne, and French theses know no limits to structuralist subjects; there is a study of the structure of Freud's punctuation.

Certainly the mode of analysis Lévi-Strauss gives us as a model is bound to enrich both anthropology and other subjects in a vigorous and wonderful way. It is a discipline which he invented, using ideas from Jakobson and Saussure, Rousseau and Frazer; a study of the forces flowing through him would sound like the intellectual history of Europe. And yet he resists being the front of a movement (what movement would it be?), as he has no ideology to promote, no body of knowledge that anyone except anthropologists can master, no theory about humanity to be thinned into a facile vulgarity. He is, I think, most like Montaigne, in that his writing is the essence of restless, intelligent, endless inquiry. He is deliciously French (like Simenon, he is a transplanted Belgian) in his abrupt put-downs, his fidgety rages (read him on India and his British disciples), and his passion for the exotic.

He is not an easy writer. *The Elementary Structures of Kinship* is one of the most difficult books ever. *The Savage Mind* is, in its charming way, almost as difficult. The four volumes of the *Mythologies* require dedication and stamina to read all 2,500 pages. Yet he has never written an uninteresting sentence. He exemplifies a remark he makes in this book, that in the study of man, there is nothing that we dare consider trivial or incidental.

What Are Those Monkeys Doing?

MEADOWS

Impressionism kept its innermost purpose a secret, being unaware of it: the idea of roads. There is scarcely an Impressionist canvas without a road, a river, a path. Locomotives appear in the unlikeliest places, behind mothers and daughters, in the far background of idyllic country scenes. It is true that roads were safe for the first time in European history, that commerce was expanding as never before.

Monet begins with the sea on the channel coast, moves on to the lovely roads cut through forests, train stations (St. Lazare was where you took the train to Vernon, and from there to Giverny), boats, harbors, cathedrals (way stations for the spirit). And then his study began to go backward in time. European agriculture is a matter of draining marshes to get a meadow. Before he turned to the primal marsh for his final great study, Monet painted meadows, haystacks, country rivers, poppy-filled fields. And with him, Renoir, Pissarro, van Gogh.

Of all the painters of meadows, Henri Rousseau was the most poetic. Dora Vallier is right to call him "the Master of the Trees," but in front of the trees are the meadows, flowery, bright with flat sunlight.

A meadow is the transition between forest and city. Rousseau spent his years as a collector of tariffs on farm produce at the old gates of Paris, where the city becomes meadow and farmland.

His career begins with the forest as a romantic place, where revelers dressed in commedia dell'arte costumes stroll under a white moon. He progresses toward the greatest of love affairs with French trees, particularly the acacia (his symbol of femininity) and the chestnut (masculinity), and, after his discovery of the hothouses in the Jardin des Plantes, the jungle, or primaeval forest. And here he made himself not only one of the greatest painters of our time, but one of the greatest poets.

FATE

His most telling self-portrait is of himself as a jumping jack dangled by a child standing in a meadow, under an acacia. A chestnut stands in the middle ground, and behind it, a road. Beyond the road, a forest. The child symbolizes innocence, the jumping jack buffoonery. All add up to Rousseau's human condition: a squabble inside him of the childlike and the foxlike. The child has gathered flowers in the meadow, and has them in a fold of its dress: the artist appropriating and presenting Beauty. And yet the child must at the same time manipulate a toy, a Punchinello. The soul and its puppet, the body. The ideal and the real. Rousseau's great talent as a painter was such a problem: he had the vision. The means for accomplishing the vision were as intractable as a floppy, obstinate doll. The child's eyes are defiant. The meadow is a paradise. Acacia and chestnut stand guard.

THE ACHIEVEMENT

But, before we get further, the triumph. He hangs in the Louvre. He never doubted that he would. He was utterly alone in that belief. He also hangs in Prague, London, New York, Moscow. Soviet dogma, tedious at best in its artistic exclusiveness, takes him to heart. Of his contemporaries, all but a few would have been outraged to know that the world would come to consider him a master, to be spoken of in the same breath as Sassetta. The settling of history's dust is always full of surprises: Emily Dickinson, John Clare, Melville. Reputations change: The eighteenth century's Kit Smart, psalmist, drunkard, and lunatic, is not our Christopher Smart, author of the *Jubilate Agno*. Our Mark Twain, the author of *Huckleberry Finn* and *Life on the Mississippi*, is not the Mark Twain of his lifetime, author of *Tom Sawyer* and *Innocents Abroad*.

Henri Rousseau's metamorphosis from a divine fool who painted laughable daubs to a painter of immense stature is an aesthetic transformation we do not yet fully understand.

QUESTIONS

His paintings refuse to age. They grow in interest. *The Sleeping Gypsy*, not known until a decade after his death (stored as junk in the basement of the prefecture at Laval), belongs to our age all the more poignantly because we do not deserve it. None of the fanatic energies of our century (capitalism, communism, fascism) could have called it into being. Violence stands poised to kill the imagination, which is defenseless. Notice the absence of trees.

DAS BEDEUTUNGSPROBLEM

Of *Les joyeux farceurs* (1906, Philadelphia Museum of Art: Louise and Walter Arensberg Collection), Yann le Pichon writes: "In his painting *Joyous Jokesters*, Rousseau depicted monkeys scratching themselves and knocking over a bottle of milk; he also gave them anthropomorphic faces."[1] They are not monkeys but gibbons, who are apes; they are not scratching themselves; they are not knocking over a bottle of milk; and God, not Rousseau, gave them anthropomorphic faces. Carolyn Keay: "This strange painting, with an upturned milk bottle and a back-scratcher in a jungle setting . . ."[2] La Keay again: "What could Rousseau have meant in *Les joyeux farceurs* (Merry jesters) [*sic*] by placing an upturned milk bottle and a backscratcher in a jungle scene which for once is peaceful and serene? There is no understandable motivation for any of these situations."[3] That's still not a milk bottle, and the motivation is perfectly understandable if you look at the picture. Jean Bouret: "Exhibited at the 1906 Salon d'Automne, this was one of the works that Maître Guilhermet produced in court to illustrate his client's naivety. The composition is beautifully proportioned: the broad leaves frame the picture at right and left; the white yucca flower at left is balanced by the vividly colored bird sitting on a branch at right; the two monkeys—the jesters—huddle together in the center foreground. The canvas is filled with a mass of carefully painted leaves in varying shades of greens and greys, yet the impression is one of depth rather than suffocating confusion."[4] There are five "monkeys," not two. All the leaves are green, none grey. Alfred Werner: "In many of Rousseau's jungle scenes, wild beasts are depicted attacking natives or weaker animals. This painting, however, offers a view of silent concord and amity: the creatures pose in complete harmony amidst the unspoiled primordial landscape. But what is the meaning of the inverted milk bottle, spilling its contents? Or of the back scratcher?"[5]

Rousseau, who said of Matisse's painting that if it was going to be ugly it at least ought to be amusing, was eminently a dramatic artist. His paintings

[1] Yann le Pichon, *The World of Henri Rousseau*, trans. Joachim Neugroschel (New York: Viking, 1982), 167.
[2] Carolyn Keay, *Henri Rousseau: Le Douanier* (London: Academy Editions, 1976), p. 20.
[3] Ibid., 30.
[4] Jean Bouret, *Rousseau* (New York: Fawcett; Greenwich Editions, 1963), 54.
[5] Alfred Werner, *Rousseau/Dufy* (New York: Tudor, 1970), 30.

Merry Jesters (Joyeux Farceurs) by Henri Rousseau.

have plots that range from the hilarious to the sublime. Before *La bohémi-enne endormie* we are meant to feel the *frisson* of realizing that the gypsy is *not* asleep; the eyes are open a minim, watching the lion; the gypsy in terror is pretending to be dead, knowing that lions eat only live prey. Will the lion see through the ruse, or will it move on? There is no hope of help. Only the indifferent moon gazes down. The lion, like the cats of Paris, has raised his tail in curiosity. Will the gypsy ever again play Hungarian airs on that man-dolin, or drink from that water jug? See how gay and bright the coat of the gypsy is! Are we not reminded of Joseph in Scripture, whose blood stained coat of many colors was brought by his wicked brothers to his grief-stricken father, as evidence that "an evil beast hath devoured him?" Pity and terror! You must realize it all in your imaginations, *messieurs et dames*. For senti-ment, could Bouguereau have done better?

Until we are willing to enter Rousseau's world we are going to misread all his paintings. We must learn the tone of his sentimentality, his sense of hu-mor, his idea of art. In *Les joyeux farceurs* we are in the comic world of *Tar-tarin de Tarascon* (1872), the Mr. Pickwick of France. Rousseau, knowing that his imaginary jungle realm admits of comedy as well as wonder and beauty, was aware of explorers in it, who when not botanizing, tracing rivers to their sources, converting the natives, and being eaten by lions and croco-diles, must have had their light moments. Let us posit a lugubrious British explorer, deep in Africa. Having set up camp for the evening, he has a scotch and soda. That's his syphon bottle in the painting. Rousseau has carefully made the bottle identifiable by its depressor shaft. He has not had any luck with the carbonated spray which the gibbons have frightened themselves with, just before being further hacked by the untimely return of the explorer from his bath in the river, or relieving his bladder.

The gibbons have perhaps watched the explorer from a distance before he stepped away momently. They have seen him scratch his back (who but a British explorer, to a Frenchman's mind, would take a backscratcher on an expedition?), spray soda water into his whisky, and, being *singes*, they must live up to their immemorial comic reputation of aping. So they inspect the explorer's walking stick, try his backscratcher, and skeet each other with fizzing water. Delicious comedy! But, that's not all—they're caught at their mischief. That's the moment of the painting. See the tall leaves parted right and left by the explorer's foot. The gibbons drop the bottle and the back-scratcher. The rightmost gibbon is still poking his fellow with the explorer's stick. Which way must we run to be saved? All eyes are on us, and on the explorer, including those of the bird in the tree.

CHARM

Personality, unlike character, is fractal. Its contours cannot be mapped, for in deciding upon the precision with which we should draw, we betray a preconception. Mandelbrot's theory is that the more particular we are in depicting a coastline, the longer it gets on a map. A man walking along a coastline with a pedometer measures a much shorter boundary than would a trained ant.

An artist can draw in outline (Lascaux, Greek vase decoration, Flaxman, Picasso) or in rich mimesis of chiaroscuro, texture, perspective (Leonardo, Ford Madox Brown). Personality, or charm, controls the former, and is its residual impression—we recognize a style of drawing as we recognize handwriting. Character controls the latter, in which meaning resides in the degree of visual resolution. Rembrandt's pathos, Braque's sincerity, Titian's voluptuousness, Leonardo's metaphysical curiosity, Vermeer's knowledge of the psychology of space: all are statements made with attitudes inherent in style. The glossy triviality of Dalí is evident everywhere in the pointless and futile finish of his canvases. In van Gogh we can follow the work of the painter, and feel the movements of hand and shoulder, keeping the moment of painting as one of its qualities.

Rousseau's charm comes across before his character. He has both in great measure. He does not, as we might expect, have lines. He makes a line happen, as in nature, by arranging the finest contrast between contingent colors.

In the *Adam and Eve* (John Hay Whitney Collection, New York) the visual resolution is as in a Leonardo, but without chiaroscuro except just enough to give volume to bodies and trees. The composition, as Dora Vallier has noted,[6] is from Leon Gérôme's *Innocence* (1852), which is a Romantic diversion of neoclassicism (naked girl and boy, fawn and a statue of Cupid above a fountain between them, style highly finished and academic). Rousseau did not have available to him the pedantic sentiment that informs Gérôme, but he had a ready Christian context, and translated them into Adam and Eve. The fawn he made into a dog, howling comically because Adam has hit a sensitive note on his flute. And so we are to be amused by the dog's howling along. Cupid has been rendered back into flesh. We are to understand him as Cain or Abel as an infant, or as Cupid. He holds one end of a vine which Eve is messing around with, making herself fortuitously decent. The painting has many good harmonies: the spray of reeds by Adam suggests the spray of notes from his flute. The dog is wearing a collar: if civilization

[6]Dora Vallier, *Henri Rousseau* (New York: Harry N. Abrams, n.d.), plate 75.

The Happy Quartet (Adam and Eve) by Henri Rousseau.

has advanced in Rousseau's Eden as far as textiles for Adam's sash, a flute and the art of music, Eve's hairdo in a bun, shaving (Adam is beardless), why not dog collars?

Question: is the painting sheer fun? Is it a conscious criticism of Gérôme? How much religious sentiment are we to read into the painting? "It is paradise," might have been all we could have got from Rousseau. Are we left with the exquisiteness of the trees, one already in autumn gold, two still green, the sweet path under the wood's edge, the clarity of the Bois de Boulogne about it all?

A ROUSSEAU BY RIMBAUD

Sur la place taillée en mesquines pelouses,
Square où tout est correct, les arbres et les fleurs,
Tous les bourgeois poussifs qu'étranglent les chaleurs
Portent, les jeudis soirs, leur bêtises jalouses.

—L'orchestre militaire, au milieu du jardin,
Balance ses schakos dans la *Valse des fifres*:
—Autour, aux premiers rangs, parade le gandin;
La notaire pend à ses breloques à chiffres.

Des rentiers à lorgnons soulignent les couacs:
Les gros bureaux bouffis traînent leurs grosses dames
Auprès desquelles vont, officieux cornacs,
Celles dont les volants ont des airs de réclames;

Sur les bancs verts, des clubs d'épiciers retraités
Qui tisonnent le sable avec leur canne à pomme,
Fort sérieusement discutent les traités,
Puis prisent en argent, et reprennent: «En Somme!. . .»

Épatant sur son banc les rondeurs de ses reins,
Un bourgeois à boutons clairs, bedaine flamande,
Savoure son onnaing d'où le tabac par brins
Déborde—vous savez, c'est de la contrebande;—

Le long des gazons verts ricanent les voyous;
Et, rendus amoureux par le chant des trombones,
Très naïfs, et fumant des roses, les pioupious
Caressent les bébés pour enjôler les bonnes. . . .

To the square by the station, with its stingy patches of grass, its trees and flowerbeds laid out so correctly, the solid citizens, short of breath from the heat, which they say is suffocating, bring their mean-minded stupidities every Thursday evening.

The military band in the middle of the park nods its shakos to the *Waltz of the Fifes:* around it the village swell shows off, along with the notary, who swings like his own watch chain.

Landlords, peering through pince-nez, criticise the band's sour notes; balloon-shaped petty bureaucrats roll along with their fat wives in tow; and behind them, like busybody elephant-drivers, women who look like department-store ads.

Retired grocers and their cronies sit on the green benches and draw in the sand with their walking sticks, quietly talking business, pinching snuff from silver boxes, saying, "What it comes to . . ."

His big behind flattened out over all the bench, a glass-buttoned Flemish-bellied shop-owner enjoys his pipe, shreds of tobacco hanging from it, good black-market tobacco, don't you know?

And along the grass borders snicker punks; and, feeling sexy because of the trombones, with childish candor the recruits smell the roses and chuck children under the chin to strike up conversations with their nursemaids . . .

(At which point, for the remaining three stanzas, Rimbaud obtrudes, and the illusion of a scene by Rousseau disappears. But for six stanzas Rimbaldian satire as robust as a Flemish genre painting has coincided detail by detail with Rousellian exactitude of observation. Rousseau would have been most interested in the color of the military band as a civic ornament in the Place de la Gare, Charleville, and in the deployment of solid citizens and pretty girls under the chestnut trees. Rimbaud's acid eye is guided by the precision of his sense of humor. Rousseau's eye, studiously compliant to the reality before him, would have been guided by a sense of humor radically different. But the comedy of the scene would have survived intact, if Rousseau had painted it.)

A ROUSSEAU BY FLAUBERT

Comme il faisait une chaleur de trente-trois degrés, le boulevard Bourdon se trouvait absolument désert.

Plus bas le canal Saint-Martin, fermé par les deux écluses, étalait en ligne droite son eau couleur d'encre. Il y avait au milieu un bateau plein de bois, et sur la berge deux rangs de barriques.

Au delà du canal, entre les maisons que séparent des chantiers, le grand ciel pur se découpait en plaques d'outremer, et, sous la réverbération du soleil, les façades blanches, les toits d'ardoises, les quais de granit éblouissaient. Une rumeur confuse montait au loin dans l'atmosphère tiède; et tout semblait engourdi par le désoeuvrement du dimanche et la tristesse des jours d'été.

Deux hommes parurent.

L'un venait de la Bastille, l'autre du Jardin des Plantes. Le plus grand, vêtu de toile, marchait le chapeau en arrière, le gilet déboutonné et sa cravate à la main. Le plus petit, dont le corps disparaissait dans une redingote marron, baissait la tête sous une casquette à visière pointue.

Quand ils furent arrivés au milieu du boulevard, ils s'assirent, à la même minute, sur le même banc.

Because the thermometer read 33 degrees [90 Fahrenheit], the Boulevard Bourdon was without traffic or pedestrians.

Further along, between two locks, ran the St. Martin canal as straight as a ruler and black as ink. Dead center in it, there was a barge loaded with wood, and along it, two rows of casks.

Beyond the canal, between buildings and lumberyards, the large clear sky was partitioned into squares of blue, and under the trembling hot sunlight white walls, slate roofs, and granite docks shone bright. A muffled noise came through the heavy heat, and everything seemed dull in the Sunday stillness and summer quiet.

Then two men came along.

One was walking from the Place de la Bastille, the other from the zoo. The taller one, wearing a linen suit, had pushed his hat to the back of his head, unbuttoned his collar, and was carrying his necktie in his hand. The smaller, who was encased in a red coat, wore a cap and walked with his head down.

In the middle of the boulevard, they came to a bench at the same time, and sat.

The opening paragraphs of *Bouvard et Pécuchet*. We feel both Joyce and Beckett. That would be Bloom from the direction of the Botanical Gardens, and his thoughts would be running on the cruelty (or kindness, with benefit to science) of keeping animals in cages, on the educational value of a great park with plants from all over the world. Rousseau was already painting such views of the canal, with figures and barges, with exactly the same tone of hot, melancholy Sunday afternoons when these lines were written. The usefulness of knowing that Flaubert and Rousseau saw the Canal Saint-Martin with the same eyes is immense. It means that we can suspect a field of pressure points, each insignificant and of trivial importance in itself, amounting in aggregate to a matrix. One such point would be a thermometer reading rather than a rhetorical figure. Another would be (as happens again in *Ulysses*) that the setting is Paris. This assumption was well established by 1880; Zola's *Thérèse Raquin* (1867) begins by telling us that we can find the Passage du Pont-Neuf at the end of the rue Guénégaud, and that it is an alley connecting the rue Mazarine and the rue de Seine. The word Paris does not turn up for forty pages. Another would be Flaubert's careful attention to color, and then to clothing, its style and capacity to place his figures as to class. The rows of barrels get into many Rousseaux, as do the barges. The scene is flat, dull, bland. Neither Flaubert nor Rousseau feel any need to impose the picturesque (Canaletto's first concern), the metaphysical (de Chirico), the touristic (Utrillo), or any other note. Balzac would have explained the worker's Sunday in Paris to us, Camus the existential anguish of it all, Sartre the seediness. Rousseau and Flaubert simply record, and hold to a faith, wholly new in art, that the scene has its meaning inherent in it. Flaubert worked in ironic disillusionment, Rousseau in the innocent belief that a depiction of the perfectly ordinary was deeply interesting because of the medium, painting: distiller of essences, negator of time, appreciator of charm, identifier of beauty, creator of wonder and civilized attention.

A ROUSSEAU BY APOLLINAIRE

Sur la côte du Texas
Entre Mobile et Galveston il y a
Un grand jardin tout plein de roses
Il contient aussi une villa
Qui est une grande rose

Une femme se promène souvent
Dans le jardin toute seule
Et quand je passe sur la route bordée de tilleuls
Nous nous regardons

Comme cette femme est mennonite
Ses rosiers et ses vêtements n'ont pas de boutons
Il en manque deux à mon veston
La dame et moi suivons presque le même rite

On the Texas coast between Mobile and Galveston there is a fine rose garden and in it a house that is also a rose

A woman often walks in the garden all alone and when I pass by on the country road lined with linden trees we take notice of each other

She's a Mennonite and her rose bushes and dress have no buttons and as my coat has lost two she and I are almost of the same religion

Rousseau would not see the playful simplicity as imitative of his effects, but he would appreciate the delicacy of the hint: that if this lady were to marry Apollinaire, and be a dutiful wife, he would not have buttons missing from his *veston*. Subtlety, *messieurs dames*, is all. And the lindens and roses are correct.

FOLKLORE

In the melodramatic *Unpleasant Surprise* (Barnes Foundation) a handsome young hunter shoots a bear who is menacing a nude woman. Her clothes are draped over the limbs of a large linden tree by a lake. Has she stripped to bathe, or has the bear through some folklorish means forced her to undress? The linden appears wherever Rousseau places a wife or mistress; Marie Laurencin stands under one in the double portrait with Apollinaire, who stands under the poetic acacia. The theme is parallel to St. George and the Dragon, but would seem to have even deeper roots in French folklore.

A seasonal festival in the Pyrenees features a bear who wakes after his winter's sleep and comes into the village to claim a human bride. He is given one; there is a wedding; and the bear is shot after he has consummated the marriage. Violet Alford, the distinguished folklorist who studied animal rituals throughout Europe, seeing them as vestiges of neolithic religions, interprets this wedding and death as symbolizing the rebirth of the year at winter's end. Rousseau probably had much folklore of this sort in mind. For all his citified sophistication, Rousseau is rarely distant from folk narrative. What he was after with all his work was a buzz of interest, talk, the generation of texts. Ironically, what we got was anecdotes (a good half of them suspect) about the man, not the work. We have a debt to pay Rousseau.

ST. JEROME WITH LION

The cat of Pierre Loti. *Hippolyte on l'appelle.*
A sardine of paleological silver the great artist
Gave him when he sat for his portrait, aromatic

And with the *soupçon* of *huile d'olive* about it,
As was proper, whose family reached back
To Nilotic tax collectors in porcelain wigs,
To the bee gums of Beersheba, Akkadian hotels,
(A cousin removed was friend to Mr Smart the poet);
Leo Alektor kept the high gates at Mycenae.
Quite Hebraic, the family tree, rich in detail.
But we are companion to Monsieur Loti.

The cat of Pierre Loti are we. We are civilization.
Our tribe has resided beyond the borders of France.
Mr Rousseau, master in the modern manner,
Has depicted us in forests of flowers, inquisitive
As catfish, intelligent as Miss Gertrude Stein.
Under starlight we have sniffed the desert arab;
Aztec vegetables and Perelandrian trees
Have been our precincts, and the gardens of Tchad.
But in *footballeurs* idiotic with motion
We take our delight, in Gruyère and sincerity,
Innocence, *bicyclettes*, Apollinaire, industry.

These stanzas from my *Flowers and Leaves* are preceded by one describing the memorabilia-lined Victorian interior bristling with disguised erotic emblems, and followed by one of similar Ernst-like imagery (airless rooms, Pompeii under ash, industrial smog). I was suggesting that Rousseau cuts through the fin-de-siècle like a green belt through a traffic-ridden city. In his portrait of Loti the smoking factory chimney is in the deep background (as in Seurat's *Bathers at Asnières*, and as distant trains traverse the horizons of some of Monet's and Renoir's most idyllic landscapes), and a tree stands between.

The French achieved an elegance and brightness of private rooms in the nineteenth century surpassing those of Naples in the eighteenth and those of Roman villas in classical times. But of these Rousseau knew nothing. He places Joseph Brummer and Apollinaire in parks, not in the rooms where Monet or Bonnard would have painted them. Where is Pierre Loti? On a balcony overlooking factories and the homes of factory workers? Standing in a field?

Space for Rousseau was the outside, never the room. Is this another reason

Portrait of Pierre Loti by Henri Rousseau.

that he disliked Matisse, who placed all his subjects in rooms (or empty exterior space which can never be taken for the out-of-doors)? Notice how many times Rousseau transplants interior furniture to the outside: a woman on a sofa in a jungle in *The Dream*, himself in a chair in a park in *Henri Rousseau as Orchestra Conductor*, Brummer in his living-room chair under trees.

BALZAC OR REMBRANDT

Novelist who changed locale and tone of weather and landscape with every novel, traveller who had been to the real jungles (Tahiti, Africa) of Rousseau's dream forests, newly elected member of the Academy, naval officer, Pierre Loti (exotic *nom de plume* symbolized by the red fez and Turkish cigarette) poses with superb confidence. The contemplative eyes are certainly Loti's, as is the moustache. A versatile doubleness controls all the themes in this painting. The man is (like Rousseau) both military and artistic, Lt. Louis-Marie-Julien Viaud, age forty-one, of the French Navy. In fez or burnous, in tents where he can hear the growl of lions and the nicker of zebras, he is a writer of romances in which handsome smugglers and virile sailors risk their lives for a night of love.

With generosity and friendliness he shares his portrait with his cat, who is as conscious of being immortalized in paint as Loti. It is only their due, this attention of a great artist, to be followed by the world's admiration when the portrait is exhibited in the Louvre. Animal and human together always make a pairing of great significance in Rousseau.

And yet a journalist and minor writer, Edmond Frank, remembered years later posing for this portrait, along with his cat, a stray from the alley that had taken up with him. Clearly what happened was that Rousseau painted Frank, and then decided that Loti was the more popular subject, and assigned the portrait to him.

Once, when Picasso was drawing caricatures in the Closerie des Lilas, he identified a face as "Balzac—or Rembrandt."

STYLE

Tradition is a genetic code. Its persistence in a culture certifies its function, however tacit that function is. We have only inadequate ideas as to why still life flourishes more in one age than another. We do know that all persistence is evolutionary, and that evolution is critical. We can point to stages in an evolution where a sudden need for vitality becomes crucial, as when an architect changes the style of houses and public buildings, or a composer changes tone and tempo in music, or painters change the subject matter of pictures. Henri Rousseau's attention to tradition was oftentimes inadvertent, we might as well say accidental, in ways that Joyce's or Baudelaire's never was. His feeling for traditional iconography was as alert as Picasso's or Klee's, both of whom were willing to act as if they were primitive artists. When Picasso changed styles, he knew exactly what he was doing; he knew his sources and the risk he was taking. Rousseau did not: this is wonderfully

useful to our knowledge of how tradition combines innovation and rules
from the past to invent new forms. The styles of Racine and Milton can be
accounted for with something like genetic formulae. Even a style as complex
and articulate as Monet's can be charted with more success than we would
have suspected at the outset. The elements of Monet's style are available to
us. The elements of Rousseau's style send us off our familiar scholarly paths,
and open up explorations.

L'ECOLE ROUSSEAU

The red sun discs of the jungle pictures, the cold white moon of *The Sleeping
Gypsy*, the hothouse foliage, and the sense that art is a dream about reality
rather than a transcription go into Max Ernst.

From the *Myself: Portrait-Landscape* Robert Delaunay took the lower
left quarter (yacht with signal flags, bridge, houses) and two of the clouds,
the ones resembling flying geese, for his large canvas *The City of Paris*. He
put Rousseau's Wright Flyer into his *Cardiff Team*, itself an homage to Rousseau's *Joueurs de Football*. Delaunay's eclecticism of style is instructive. In
The City of Paris he translates a Renaissance motif into cubist idiom with
the same wit and freshness as Apollinaire using traditional poetic forms for
contemporary subjects. The borrowing of Rousseau demonstrates an architectural sureness: yacht and bridge occupy the same space without any
crowding or muddle. But Rousseau has made a harmony of bridge, yacht,
and Eiffel Tower. Delaunay moved the red tower to the right of his composition.

Peter Blake's *Self-Portrait with Badges* (1961) is an homage to Rousseau's
landscape-portrait. How the world has changed.

PRIMITIVE

Grove's Dictionary defined Charles Ives as a primitive composer up to the
present edition. In Amsterdam around 1963 I remember seeing Edwin Ro-
manzo Elmer's *Mourning Picture* (1890) in a show of primitive painters. I
would more readily concede primitiveness to all the novels of the Brontës and
the architecture of the Crystal Palace than to Ives or Elmer.

Early Balthus displays as many signs of the primitive as Rousseau; both
painters were self-taught. A Martian observer might well consider Picasso,
not Rousseau, our modern primitive.

Rousseau's style is a dialect, like Joel Chandler Harris' Black Georgia English, of which he and Brer Rabbit are masters, or the Scots of Burns. We
cannot check grammar or diction against a rulebook. We can admire its ar-

ticulateness, verve, and success and can only compare it to itself. It is therefore a privileged style, as Degas' is not, where standards set by Michelangelo and Leonardo are being kept to. The first page of *Ulysses* is meant to vie with Flaubert, just as a Cézanne is confident of holding its own against a Poussin. Rousseau, for all his subtle quotations (the leftmost fallen figure in *War*, the animals in the jungle pictures, the virgin in *The Holy Family*), is Brer Rabbit all the way. His qualities that bear comparison—the Pierre Loti with Memling's *Portrait of a Man* (Florence), the still life of coffeepot and candle with Zurbarán, the *Sleeping Gypsy* with Gérôme—are all accidental parallels.

FOURIER

The Henri Rousseau of French philosophy.

ACCURACY

Rousseau's remark to Picasso, "We are the greatest living painters, I in the modern, you in the Egyptian manner," was absolutely accurate.

TRADITION

The Gaulish attempts at Roman sculpture (as at St.-Germain-en-Laye) which came out in a style we call primitive begin a long tradition. Rousseau belongs to that tradition, at least, if to no other.

GENIUS

What, psychologically, was most useful to Rousseau was not childishness but a quality wholly mature: the ability to fool himself. In a lifetime of supposing he had achieved what most mature people achieve (as Ibsen shows us in all his plays), an inaccurate and fictional idea of themselves and their world, Rousseau certainly saw his paintings as he wanted to see them, as academically finished as Bouguereau or Rosa Bonheur. In this he was a kind of Don Quixote; and as with the Don, Rousseau wins us over to his way of seeing.

VINDICATIONS

A good case can be made for Rousseau as the best draughtsman of his age. Picasso could never get style out of his drawing. Rousseau could. Things themselves, tigers, flags, canals, moons, got into his paintings in styles they themselves demanded.

Primitive painters are usually realists, devoted to the literal visually and to some ideal thematically. They are true poets in that they know no ordinariness, insisting on the right of what they see to be in a painting. Shelley probably could not see a kettle, a chair, a pair of shoes.

A tree was as important a presence for Rousseau as an angel for Joan of Arc.

SEURAT

La Grande Jatte and the *Bathers at Asnières* are motifs thoroughly suited to Rousseau, and there is an uncanny resemblance of staging, distance, deployment of figures. The background of the Asnières painting is hauntingly Rousseau-like. They are equally formalistic, Rousseau and Seurat, while being at opposite poles from each other. Rousseau's surfaces are all enamelled, or ceramic, or like painted wood. Seurat's surface is the Brownian movement of light.

Newtonian physics, the French ground of nature from Voltaire to Fourier (with grand moments in between: Boullée's cenotaph, libraries, stadium, all as solid as Gibraltar or the buildings in Poussin's imaginary Rome and Athens) has its last assertion in Rousseau. Impressionist light is Einsteinian, an omnidirectional halo (as Leonardo had said), vibrant, fugitive, splendid.

Rousseau's light is polarized, inert, static. It comes from within things. His trees are self-lit.

BONHEUR

About the time Rousseau painted the *Football Players* (1906), the Baron Coubertin, founder of the modern Olympics, was lecturing on the return of grace to the body, and rude health to schoolboys. The essence of Hellenism, he said, was *bonheur* (which we ought to translate as *delight* or *joy* rather than *happiness*), a state of inner harmony, a sensuality of well-being. The FIFA (Fédération Internationale de Football Association) was founded in Paris in May 1904. Coubertin wanted a soccer field in the Bois de Boulogne. He was given one. It had trees in it. Coubertin said that the trees must be removed. The city fathers said that his schoolboys could play their silly game among the trees, which they were not going to cut down. That is why Rousseau's players (the game is rugby; the ball is oval) are hemmed in by trees. Chestnuts, the masculine tree. Gentleman at play in the English manner, deep in the modern *bonheur*, details of which were flying in a machine (Rousseau is the first to paint an airplane, the Wright Flyer No.2, exhibited at Le Mans, 1909), exploring jungles, riding to the country in the grocer Junier's cart, together with his family and dogs.

The nineteenth century had triumphed over all the ages, and was filling the world with *bonheur*. "But why has Robert broken the Tour Eiffel?" he asked on his deathbed.

Rousseau's *War* hangs in the Louvre.

Transcendental Satyr

Ancient Greek poets wrote without spaces between their words, without capital letters, and without punctuation. The classical equivalent for memorandum paper was the pottery shard, on which notes ("The saw is under the garden bench and the gate is unlatched" says one displayed in the Museum of the Agora in Athens) were incised, shopping lists, and the text of poems. This is the way Sappho's

> Come out of Crete
> And find me here,
> Come to your grove,
> Mellow apple trees
> And holy altar
> Where the sweet smoke
> Of libanum is in
> Your praise . . .

has come down to us (Fragment 2, Lobel and Page, *Poetarum Lesbiorum Fragmenta*), fitted onto the wedge shape of the *ostrakon*. And when these early poems, none of which has survived entire but exist on torn, rotted, rat-gnawn papyrus or parchment, are set in type for the modern student of Greek, such as Edward Estlin Cummings, Greek major at Harvard (1911–1916), the text is a frail scatter of *lacunae*, conjectures, brackets, and parentheses. They look, in fact, very like an E. E. Cummings poem. His eccentric margins, capricious word divisions, vagrant punctuation, *tmeses*, and promiscuously embracing parentheses, can be traced to the scholarly trappings which a Greek poem wears on a textbook page. Cummings' playfulness in writing a word like "l(oo)k"—a pair of eyes looking from inside the word— must have been generated by the way scholars restore missing letters in botched texts, a Greek *l[oo]k*, where the *l* and *k* are legible on a papyrus, there's space for two letters between them, and an editor has inserted a conjectural *oo*.

And *i* for *I*, Cummings' trademark. To make a delicious symmetry in literary history, one would like to think that when Don Marquis invented in 1916 a cockroach named archy, a *vers libre* poet in a previous incarnation, who could type but couldn't manage the shift bar for capital letters, he was having fun in his *New York Sun* column with one E. E. Cummings, whose first poems appeared that year in *Eight Harvard Poets*. But none of Cummings' poems in that volume has the mannerisms Marquis is satirizing (there was an *i* but the proofreader corrected it to *I*), and the matter seems to be the other way around. Cummings was influenced by Don Marquis, who was then parodying whom? Eventually, in one of the perfect pairings of illustrator and author in all of history, George Herriman, the creator of Krazy Kat (under whose spell Cummings had already fallen by 1916, and would remain there the rest of his life, so that we can appreciate a lot of Cummings by remembering that at any moment in any of his poems he is likely to be ventriloquizing the elate Krazy), would give us images of archy and mehitabel.

Donald Robert Perry Marquis (of Walnut, Illinois) had come to New York newspaper work by way of a stint under Joel Chandler Harris on the *Atlanta Journal*, bringing a rich measure of the animal fable with him. We first see the animal fable in the Greek poet Archilochos, whose fragments (and satiric wit and erotic sensibility) Cummings studied at Harvard. So we can see a pattern at the beginning of Cummings' career. By heritage as a young poet he had before him the bearded bards of his native Cambridge, Longfellow, Lowell, and Company, and the poets they claimed descent from, Tennyson, the Elizabethans, Dante. But quite early we can see Cummings ducking these official voices and going for the rebels. He discovered Pound and intuited what he was up to. His friend J. Sibley Watson introduced him to Rimbaud, Verlaine, and Mallarmé. Cummings seems to have invented himself out of a set of choice influences: the Greek lyric, the comic strip Krazy Kat, Don Marquis, Pound's array of resurrected Provençal, Italian, Greek, and even Chinese lyricists, some modern French poets (Apollinaire, Mallarmé), and his temperamental disposition to love and hate the world (*odi et amo*), the ambiguous and versatile stance of the satiric poet down through western tradition, from Archilochos through Catullus to Villon, and in folk tradition from Aesop to Joel Chandler Harris. Add one more element, and we have Cummings' worktable before us. Add the *mimiambus*, or mime for a single actor taking various roles. This is the tradition in which Cummings did some of his finest work. In "ygUDuh/ ydoan/ yunnuhstan . . ." he is miming a New Yorker at a bar giving his opinion of why the Second World War is being fought. He could do a Cambridge townie pretending to confuse the sex of a Harvardling, gangsters, New England farmers, genteel lady poets, anybody at all. I would put this gift for mimicry as the bedrock of Cummings' talent. When he strayed from it (into Swinburne and Rossetti), he was weak; when he exercised it with malicious wit, he was strong.

To insult Hemingway in a vicious epigram, he assumes the voice of Brooklyn sass:

> what does little Ernest croon
> in his death at afternoon?
> (kow dow r 2 bul retoinis
> wus de woids uf lil Oinis

A lugubrious poetic question (as maybe from Felicia Hemans) is answered in the illiterate vernacular, with idiotic lip (but nevertheless with Longfellow's "Hymn of Life" coming through the static): "Cow thou art, to bull returnest"—containing an aspersion on Hemingway's masculinity, while finding in Hemingway's *Death in the Afternoon* a sentimental continuation of American romantic regard for Spain (hence the Longfellow touch), an opinion of Hemingway's art (bullshit), and a bit of city smut about country pastures.

To insult Louis Untermeyer he made a Gilbert-and-Sullivan Catullus epigram as prickly as a briarpatch:

> mr u will not be missed
> who as an anthologist
> sold the many on the few
> not excluding mr u

Deflation by initial, an anticipated inversion of *de mortuis nil nisi bonum*, a concealed second and high-horse insult in the first line ("Mister, *you* will not be missed!"), insinuation that Untermeyer was an elitist (the many, the few, proles and aristocrats), an ambiguity in the third line that renders Untermeyer, in one slant of meaning, as exclusive in compiling his anthologies, and in another slant, as a huckster, and in yet another, as compiling anthologies that have more poets in them than readers of them. The final insult is not so much in accusing Untermeyer of including himself in his anthologies as in the coyness of Cummings' mimicked phrasing.

To insult Auden and Spender, he switches from voice to voice, from adenoidal coed to Oxford British to Bennington professor.

flotsam and jetsam

[floating trash, washed up trash; we would have to consult the shade of Martial in Hades to pick out the gibes, but don't miss "floats 'em and jets 'em," distinguishing perquisites in seduction made easy by a reputation]

> were gentlemen poeds
> urseappeal netsam
> our spinsters and coeds

[Erse appeal—Irish charm—because Yeats blazed the college circuit which arse appeal exploits? Cummings, like Shakespeare, would lose the world for a quibble]

thoroughly bretish

[as long as we're playing with vowels, "brutish" (especially as the unhyphenated "inhuman" is coming in the next line) can slip in on the coattails of "British"]

> they scout the inhuman
> itarian fetish
> that man isn't wuman

[squirm through that: it's a Freudian demon disguised as a platitude]

> vive the millenni
> um three cheers for labor
> give all things to enni
> one bugger thy nabor

[Leftist slogans, one of which is almost left out and recalled with that "um"! deteriorate, after cocktails, into jovial rascality]

> (neck and senecktie
> are gentlemen ppoyds
> even whose recktie
> are covered by lloyd's

[Latin *senecta*, old age: it was a current witticism even in 1939, when this was written, that Spender was the world's oldest promising young poet.]

Cummings' genius flourished in exact observation commented on with wit, whether puckish or blistering, skills exercised at length in *The Enormous Room*, but most effectively in his Russian travel diary, *EIMI*, a book that repays the patience its reading requires.[1] His genius tended to lose control when it attempted whimsy and Marcel-Marceau-like feyness ("there's a hell/ of a good universe next door; let's go"—which is meant to jolt us into realizing that death is the only alternative to life on this planet, but which comes out sounding like "stop the world, I want to get off").

The worst of Cummings is his gaily sentimental verse, in which he is the Gene Kelly of poetry. His worst fault is in scrambling typography so that poems become needlessly difficult to read and defeat being recited. He left us an enormous amount of lyric poems: 845 pages of them in the *Complete Poems* published by Harcourt Brace Jovanovich in 1962. This hefty volume tends to obliterate the fact of design in each of Cummings' books, all of which are cleverly symmetrical in one way or another, and are strictly ordered as to sequence. I'm not happy with the series of reprints, in typescript, which George James Firmage is bringing out,[2] and yet I see the reason for them, and rejoice that he has given us *Tulips & Chimneys* as Cummings originally planned it (it got broken up into two volumes, which, put back together, still do not equal the book as planned) and, at long last, a definitive *The Enormous Room*, which was printed botched and bowdlerized in 1922.

But why typescript? Cummings was lucky in having his books designed by sensitive typographers. The care that Cummings took to shape his poems became in time a vice. Ultimately one has to set aside the *Eigendichtung* claim on our attention; the voice cannot reflect it, nor the eye read it; it is a false complication. I think it got there because modern art of any sort first struck the public as incomprehensible, whether late Monet, Cézanne, or cubism; Stravinsky, Joyce, or Pound. This dazzle effect became desirable to

[1]Books with unpronounceable titles have their own fate. Cummings' lifelong failure to be a democrat is easily detectable in his titles. You have to know that overlapping V's are the Italian grafitto for *viva*, that *eimi* is Greek and that it's one of two verbs, first person singular; with an acute accent on the final *i*, it's "I go," with a circumflex over the *ei*, it's "I am." Cummings meant both. *XAIPE* (the X a guttural *kh*, rhymes with *wiry*) is Greek for "hello."

[2]E. E. Cummings, *XAIPE*, ed. and with an afterword by George James Firmage (Liveright, 1979). E. E. Cummings, *Tulips & Chimneys*, ed. and with an afterword by George James Firmage and introduction by Richard S. Kennedy (Liveright, 1976). E. E. Cummings, *W. (VIVA)*, ed. and with an afterword by George James Firmage (Liveright, 1979). E. E. Cummings, *No Thanks*, ed. by George James Firmage and introduction by Richard S. Kennedy (Liveright, 1978).

artists (we can see Hart Crane striving for it with his baroque phrasing and big words, and John Marin with his gratuitous cubist clichés). Cummings fell into the trap of false density (his most typographically complex lyrics are also his most trivial).

He was, indeed, a man of contradictions and many conflicting energies. Richard S. Kennedy's biography[3] begins by pondering how the satyr and the Old Curmudgeon of Patchin Place lived in the same mind. He was raised in a classically liberal family—the father Harvard's first professor of sociology, and a Congregational minister to boot; the mother of staunch New England independent stock—and yet he was, first furtively, then openly, to the right of Ezra Pound. He adored sex with a sentimental enthusiasm but made a miserable husband to at least two wives, and a great deal of his machismo was in his mind only.

His childhood was idyllic, comfortable, joyful. His first word was "Hurrah!" He was raised as something between an angel and a prodigy, receiving the best education available (Agassiz School, Cambridge Latin School, Harvard B.A. and M.A.), in an ambience that honored and rewarded seriousness, good will, and intellect.

He was at Harvard just at the end of the golden period. William James, Agassiz, and Santayana were gone, but much remained. He entered Harvard as pure and idealistic as the young of *Homo sapiens* can be (but with such a rash of acne all over that he was ashamed to turn up for PT classes). By the time he left, he was a hard-drinking, womanizing, thoroughly entertaining roustabout, the despair of his parents. He clearly enjoyed shocking people, and was at great pains to see that he got the best effect. He was, to speak bluntly, a selfish prig and spoiled brat. He was also one of the most talented poets in our literature.

To recount Cummings' life to someone who cannot balance the personality with the achievement of the writer is, at the least, embarrassing. He seduced his best friend's wife, only to make a mess of his marriage to her, and did not acknowledge the daughter he begot until the daughter was a grown woman with children of her own. He idealistically (and rather blindly) joined the Norton-Harjes Ambulance Service before the USA got into the First World War (it was a fashionable thing for Harvard and Yale to do), went AWOL for weeks as soon as he arrived in France, living the good life in Paris (unable to buy the convenience of the *poules* out of sheer shyness), and when he was caught up with and commanded to report to his unit, he

[3]Richard S. Kennedy, *Dreams in the Mirror: A Biography of E. E. Cummings* (Liveright, 1980).

was faced for the first time in his protected life with common people, me-
chanics, medics, soldiers. It is shocking to know that he found them boorish,
uneducated, and revolting. His cooperation with the ambulance unit (which
existed to come to the aid of the worst carnage in the world's history) was so
poor, and his complaints so whining, that the sensible French arrested him
and quite rightly jugged him in an alien detention camp (the experience of
The Enormous Room), out of which Woodrow Wilson himself had to rescue
him.

Back in the states, he was drafted, but never saw action. The rest of his life
is one of writing and painting, with a restless moving about. It is galling in
this age of inflation to know that Cummings *had* to live half of each year in
Paris in order to keep within his means. He went to Russia (the trip was sub-
sidized: did the man ever pay for anything in his life?) and wrote *EIMI*, one
of the best travel books of our time. He lived in Patchin Place in New York,
and at the family summerhouse in New Hampshire. He painted and talked
(brilliantly, by every account), and played at being the bohemian. Prof. Kennedy explains a lot of his irresponsibility as immaturity. I would call it self-
ishness. The artistic temperament requires a great deal of what looks to the
outsider as dead time, but which is gestation periods for works of art. Joyce
appears to be something of a blackguard in Ellmann's biography for the simple reason that his art always came first with him. The artist is a kind of monster. Look at Shelley, van Gogh, Stanley Spencer, and yet art of awesome
splendor came out of their disjointed and messy lives.

Cummings was one of the most careful of poets. He drafted every poem
many times (and ironically became one of the instigators of the ripped-off
first-draft poem written nowadays by 98% of our so-called poets) and never
released a text that was not polished to perfection as he could achieve it. We
can only explain the man by noting that he was suspended helplessly between two ideals: the highly moral transcendental one of his upbringing and
the frat-house insouciance of Jazz Age spontaneity. The second, I think, was
a mask. The essential Cummings was the man whose last act (before the
heart attack on the stairs) was to sharpen the ax with which he had just split
a supply of firewood.

In his later years he gave the Charles Eliot Norton Lectures at Harvard
and went on the college reading circuit, not realizing the contempt that university faculties have for the artist, or the radical incapacity of his student
audiences to distinguish critically the poetry of Rod McKuen from that of
Christopher Marlowe. He convinced himself that Franklin *and* Eleanor

Roosevelt had ruined the country. A pacifist, he raged that we did not attack Russia during the Hungarian Revolution. He was, in effect, the usual crank the young red-bonneted rebel ages into.

One of the curiousest things about Cummings is the static course of his art. For all its excellence, it has no periods of development. It is exactly the same at the beginning as at the end. You cannot talk about Late, Middle, and Early Cummings. You can't guess when a poem was written. The Balloon Man and Buffalo Bill poems are at the very beginning of his career (half a century long); they might just as plausibly be placed toward the end. He was the greatest sonneteer of our century, though identifying the sonnets (they are everywhere) is not easy.

Not since Emily Dickinson has there been so pure a poet. True, he had a homemade philosophy about individuality that he thought he ought to push, and a sentimental regard for the put-upon (like Olaf and the man the Good Samaritan helped) which he didn't really feel. The finest Cummings is the merciless satirist and the elegist ("when god lets my body be") and the salty amorist. He is the wittiest of American poets, and must be placed among our finest craftsmen. He was not a wise person, but had the wisdom of his folly, a bravado of spirit, and his own special way of knowing and talking about the world; and these are better than wisdom, to a poet, in any choice.

Montaigne

When, in the good September weather of 1580, Michel Eyquem de Montaigne's medicine-and-book-laden coach set out for Rome by way of Austria and Switzerland and all the sights and spas along the road, Shakespeare was a loud sixteen (given to making speeches in a high style, Aubrey records) in the country town of Stratford, and Ben Jonson was a cunning little schoolboy of seven in London, learning Latin and Greek. Michelangelo had died the year Shakespeare was born. The springtime of the Renaissance was over. It was in its high summer, and its energies were moving outward from the Mediterranean. Raleigh and Drake were on the seas, copies of North's Plutarch on their cabin tables. Elizabeth, the Protestant queen of the English, who was the same age as Montaigne, had translated Boethius. A few months before his journey Montaigne had seen the first edition of the *Essais* through the press in Bordeaux.

With the *Essais* the Renaissance leaves its long period of fervent rediscovery and invention, and enters the moment when classical attitudes have become an habitual climate for the arts and education. Montaigne's first language was Latin. His mind was speculative in the manner of the Hellenistic age: eclectic in philosophy, skeptical in religion, Stoic in the conduct of life. Montaigne's emulator in the eighteenth century, the Danish humanist Ludvig Holberg, would write, "If a man learns theology before he learns to be a human being, he will never become a human being." In the travel journal we see Montaigne again and again trying to find the man beneath the theology, the human reality beneath the trappings of office and position. He admires the affable humility of an innkeeper who is also a town councilman and who abandons his civic duties to wait at table, while finding a grand duke a snob. In Ferrara he may have seen Tasso insane, and in the next edition of the *Essais* speculated on how ambition and genius can destroy the mind.

The account of a journey by a wide-awake traveller rarely fails to make good reading. In his ability to convey a sense of place with a few deft details (a topiary garden, an historical site, local anecdotes) Montaigne can be compared to Basho, whose *Journey to the Far North* is the ideal form of all journeys of passionate pilgrims to shrines and to places which they have already visited in their imagination. Other than the meditations of his contemporaries Pierre de Ronsard and Joachim du Bellay on the ruins of Rome and the remoteness in time of the Golden Age, Montaigne had no Romanticism to color his response to Italy. His eye is practical, curious, ironic.

He is, in a surprisingly modern sense, a tourist, with a tourist's interest in the amenities of the table and the bedroom. He is also, as we are never allowed to forget, a man in pain looking for a cure. His body cannot use certain minerals, such as calcium, which accumulate as pellets in his kidneys and bladder. The pain of a kidney stone is fierce, and in a male can be comparable to a woman's labor. The frequent "colic" in this journal (assuming that to be Montaigne's word for an attack of the stone) is a severe nausea in combination with the feeling that one's back is broken and that one's bowels need to move. Montaigne was fortunate in being able to pass his kidney stones. Another sufferer, Sir Walter Scott, could not, and abided pain of excruciating intensity for as long as two weeks at a time, helplessly screaming and hearing the New Testament read to him. Montaigne's constant scrutiny of his urine in a chamber pot, his colics and dizzy spells, his ability to drink heroic amounts of hot sulfurous water, locate his journal in a time when the body was still part of personality. Later, it would disappear. Dickens' characters, for instance, have no kidney stones because they have no kidneys. From Smollett to *Ulysses*, there is not a kidney in English literature.

With the occlusion of the body there is an anaesthesia of sensibilities. Montaigne's curiosity is omnidirectional. An aristocrat with inbred self-assurance, he is unhampered by the timidities that bedevil the modern tourist. With what cool aplomb does Montaigne arrange a beauty contest and a dance for young folk at a spa, inquire vigorously of Protestants their differences sect by sect, kiss the Pope's slipper, master the social ins and outs of the Roman *ricorso*, and talk with people in every level of society, from children to cardinals.

A lively conversation with a craftsman in Pisa causes an invisible event which we read over in innocence unless alerted to what's happening. When, on Saturday, 8 July 1581, Montaigne in Pisa learned "that all trees bear as many circles and rings as they have lasted years," he is recording that fact for the second time in history. Until recently, we thought it was the first time.

On this particular day he was, like any tourist, shopping for things he would probably have other thoughts about back in Bordeaux. He bought a little cask of tamarisk wood with silver hoops, a walking stick "from India," a small vase, a walnut goblet also "from India." The man who sold him these things made mathematical instruments and fine cabinets. He knew wood. We can imagine the conversation between the craftsman and the polite foreigner with such curiosity about everything. Did the French gentleman know that in a cross section of a tree trunk the number of concentric rings gives the age of the tree?

He did not, but was careful to make note of the fact. And there it is, in the essayist's journal, between a passage about a gift of fish to an acting company in Pisa and a passage about a laxative for his debilitating constipation, seemingly the first notation of a fact we might have supposed that everyone had always known. Historians of science used to assure us that until this nameless woodworker imparted the fact to Montaigne we had no evidence of it.

Ninety-two years afterwards, in one of those collisions that seem to plague scientific discoveries, the secretary of the Royal Society in London received two manuscripts of botanical studies. One was from the Italian anatomist and botanist Marcello Malpighi, the founder of modern physiology. The other was from an Englishman with the wonderful name of Nehemiah Grew. The advantage that these two Renaissance botanists had over the ancients was the microscope, and between them they added as much to information too minute for the eye as their contemporary wielders of the telescope added to information too remote. And in both their manuscripts was the fact that the rings of trees in a cross section of tree trunk tell us the tree's age.

Montaigne's recording of this fact would not be published until 1774, when the manuscript of the journal was found in a chest at the château. So Malpighi and Grew, neck and neck, beat Montaigne into print. Let's, briefly, follow this one detail of the journal into its reverberations, if only to show how Montaigne's acute and voracious attentiveness can steer us along a current of the times. Malpighi had been a professor at the University of Pisa, where he was a friend of the mathematician Giovanni Borelli. Now earlier in the century Borelli's professorship had been held by one Luca Pacioli (he invented double-entry bookkeeping, if you want something to remember him by), a friend and associate of Leonardo da Vinci. Leonardo drew the illustrations for Pacioli's geometric study *De Divina Proportione*. Leonardo's best-known drawing, that of a man with his arms and legs in two positions inside a circle and a square, derives from his work with Pacioli.

When, in 1771, subscribers to the first *Encyclopaedia Britannica* could read, in the article "Agriculture," that "annual rings, which are distinctly visible in most trees when cut through, serve as natural marks to distinguish their age," they were being given a fact culled from Nehemiah Grew's *Anatomy of Plants*, one of Johnson's authorities for the *Dictionary*. Only recently have scholars knuckled down to sorting out everything in Leonardo's extensive notebooks, new volumes of which keep turning up. The Italian scholar Antonio Baldacci noticed that Leonardo recorded, and most probably discovered, some eighty years before Montaigne had his conversation at Pisa with the maker of mathematical instruments, that a tree's age can be told from its annual rings. It would seem, as Pisa keeps bobbing up in the history of this fact, that Pacioli learned it from Leonardo, Borelli from Pacioli. Did Malpighi learn it at Pisa, or discover it on his own? Montaigne's woodworker would have learned it from one Pisan professor or another.

Thus we can trace Leonardo's "obstinate rigor of attention" (the phrase is Paul Valéry's) to one fine detail of nature as it caught the sharp eye of Montaigne. Just as we have to be alerted age after age by our own new concerns to go back to Leonardo to see if he wasn't there first, so must we reread Montaigne, the travel journal along with the inexhaustible *Essays*, with fresh eyes every generation. Fernand Braudel found a mine of information in the journal for his studies of everyday life in the sixteenth century. The historian of religion, of Renaissance Italy, of medicine, of economics—Montaigne's obstinate rigor of attention serves them all.

The emotional center of gravity of the journal is, I like to think, the day in the Vatican library when Montaigne, having gazed lovingly at a manuscript Vergil and other treasures, falls into a conversation with scholars and gentlemen about Plutarch. It was his opinion that Amyot's recent translation of the *Parallel Lives of Noble Greeks and Romans* (1559) and of the *Moralia* (1572) had "taught us all how to write." Plutarch had indeed taught Montaigne how to write. It is a common error to say that Montaigne invented the essay. Plutarch invented the essay, and wrote seventy-eight of them; Montaigne invented its name in French and English.

Renaissance, rebirth. But most of the rebirths were also transformations. Phidias is not reborn in Michelangelo, nor Ovid in Poliziano. For accuracy of regeneration we have to turn to Plutarch and Montaigne. There is an uncanny resemblance between the mayor of Chaeroneia in the first century and the mayor of Bordeaux in the sixteenth. Both retired early from public life after a thorough formal education and a taste of metropolitan business and court intrigue. In his life of Demosthenes, Plutarch notes that Greek opinion held that "the first requisite of a man's happiness is birth in a famous city." Virtue, however, can flourish anywhere, Plutarch says, and as for him, "I live in a small city, and I prefer to dwell there that it may not become smaller still." So the *Lives* and *Moralia* were written by a family man in a small town in Boeotia, and the *Essays* were written on a wine-growing estate outside Bordeaux, both by men of the most honest introspection in the history of letters, both skeptics with Stoic minds and well-tempered good natures. It has been said of Montaigne, and can be said of Plutarch, that in reading him we read ourselves.

We all lead a moral inner life of the spirit, on which religion, philosophy, and tacit opinion have many claims. To reflect on this inner life rationally is a skill no longer taught, though successful introspection, if it can make us at peace with ourselves, is sanity itself. The surest teachers of such reflection, certainly the wittiest and most forgiving, are Plutarch and Montaigne.

Montaigne's stately tomb (with effigy in marble, his *Essays* on his chest, and with the inscription in Greek, a Latin translation being provided beneath for the illiterate) is in the Municipal Building at the junction of the rue Pasteur and the cours Victor Hugo, in Bordeaux. Montaigne's even temperament and habitual affection for life in all its forms was shaped by the ancient, even prehistoric, spirit of Bordeaux, one of the most cultivated provincial towns of the Roman Empire. In its first distinguished literary figure, Ausonius (fourth century A.D.) we can make out affinities with Montaigne. He was half pagan, less than half Christian. He read everything, quoted everybody, and sported an erudition that clearly had for its message that although he lived at a great remove from Rome, Alexandria, and Athens, nevertheless we Bordelais are right up with everything. We read books. We have a university. We have travelled. We are witty and well-mannered.

Bordeaux is still a gracious, very beautiful provincial city, which has been chosen down through history to be the city to which the government in Paris retires in time of trouble. It therefore considers Paris imprudent and a bit vulgar, looking to London through ancient allegiances as its spiritual capital.

A Roman tombstone in the Museum of Aquitania states the persistent symbol of Bordeaux: a society of people and animals. This stele is a sculpture of a child holding a rooster whose tail a puppy is pulling. An hour's drive brings you to the prehistoric caves in the Val Dordogne with their murals of thousands of animals painted and engraved. A city bus takes you to Montaigne's château, where he wondered if he played with his cat or his cat with him. Bordeaux is the birthplace of Rosa Bonheur. Did she know that she was continuing the business of the painters of Lascaux? Goya died there, having restated in *The Bulls of Bordeaux* a subject native to the region for thirty thousand years. Every Bordelais has a dog for a companion. The local strays have evolved a breed over the years, the Bordeaux Dog, an affable boulevardier of considerable charm and friendliness. Every restaurant and café has its cat (even the bar at the Théâtre, where John Adams saw his first play). It is wonderful that Montaigne lies at the corner of the rue Pasteur (doctor of men and animals) and the cours Victor Hugo, whose favorite dog was named Senate. The nostalgia we feel in reading Montaigne, the sense that he was more comfortable in his world than we can ever be in ours, is in part that he knew without embarrassment the animal body in which the human spirit lives. In Switzerland we watch him listening to the doctrines of Zwingli as if he were a very intelligent horse, his common sense as unassailable by Zwingli as a mountain by a snowflake.

It is his poor animal body whose urine is full of painful sand that he takes from spa to spa on his journey. It is with a tame animal's willingness to play his master's games (sit up, roll over, heel) that he kisses the Pope's foot (thinking God knows what in the inviolable privacy of his mind). He thought for himself, Monsieur Montaigne of Bordeaux. And thought so well, so searchingly, with such wit and intelligence, that he remains for us the best example of the sane mind and liberal spirit.

Herondas

Though we knew that in ancient Greek culture there was such a thing as a *mimos*, or mime played by a single maskless actor taking all the parts, probably in city squares of an afternoon or on small stages in wineshops, it was not until 1890 that archaeology recovered a script of any of them—seven scripts, in fact, with titles native to and characteristic of the long tradition of European comedy from Aristophanes to Samuel Beckett: *The Matchmaker, The Whorehouse Manager, The Schoolmaster, Women at the Temple, The Jealous Woman, A Private Talk Between Friends, The Shoemaker,* all miraculously intact in column after column on a papyrus scroll. There are fragments of six more mimes on the same scroll, but they are too botched and torn to be made anything of. Another text for one of them (*The Dream*) was found later at Oxyrhynchus, in almost as bad a condition as the text on the scroll. The author of these playlets was a poet named Herondas, or Herodas, about whom we know nothing at all, neither his city (Kos or Alexandria, perhaps) nor when he lived (the evidence points to the third century B.C.). As for his name, its scant occurrence favors Herodas. I opt for Herondas as having a more decisive pronunciation in English.

The papyrus scroll with Herondas' mimes on it was bought in Egypt by the British Museum's diligent scout E. Wallis Budge, one of the crack buccaneers of archaeological discovery when the rules of the game were to bring home the bacon by hook or by crook. Budge bought the scroll from Coptic tomb robbers, who had filched it from the grave of some important Egyptian of the early Roman period. It was customary to await resurrection with one's library to hand. Alkman's great odes, for instance, were found in a funerary collection of this sort, as well as the text of the Egyptian Book of the Dead for which Wallis Budge is best known.

The scroll is actually the account sheets of one Didymus, a bailiff in the Roman colonial administration. Its style of handwriting, thought by Herondas' first editor to be of the first century A.D., is now considered by his most recent editor, I. C. Cunningham, who describes it as "a small, plain book-hand, with corrections by the first hand and by at least one other hand," to belong to the second century A.D. On the back of the scroll, in an economic use of good papyrus, Didymus had copied out a kind of personal anthology of choice texts: Aristotle's treatise on the Athenian constitution, the odes of Bacchylides, some orations of Hyperides, and thirteen mimes by Herondas.

It was the Aristotle that most excited the curators at the British Museum: a unique text known previously only by quotations from it by classical writers. Frederick Kenyon, the great papyrologist, transcribed and published all these texts in 1891. The classicist Walter Headlam brought out a scholarly edition of Herondas, with translation, in 1922, and this remained, until Cunningham's edition in 1971, the authoritative text. Because of his richness of diction and vividness of realism, Herondas has been the subject of much scholarship. He has not, however, enjoyed much of a reputation beyond the classicist's lamp. If, as in Cunningham's judgment he is "not an author of outstanding importance or a poet of the first rank," and if, in Frederick Will's assessment he is "the least edifying of the Hellenistic poets," he is nevertheless an abundantly interesting, superbly vigorous poet.

The first step toward seeing him as he must be seen is to imagine a performance. We live in the age of Picasso, who has given us a new vision of the classical world's acrobats, mimes, street actors and singers as they have survived through the unbroken lineage of festival, Italian comedy, the circus. The same figures who cavort at Mardi Gras throughout civilization today could be seen before Aristophanes was born—we have the evidence of painted vases to guide us here—wearing the same carnival costumes, hilarious masks, impersonating the same kind of comic types. We live in the age of Fellini, of Beckett, of Marcel Marceau. The ghost of Herondas cannot find us wholly unfamiliar. Just beyond the strangeness of his surface we can easily locate human nature as we know it all too well.

Were we Alexandrians of the third century B.C., citizens of a center of commerce and learning, a polyglot city on the Mediterranean, we would know the public mime as a matter of course. Imagine a broad, level area between buildings, with steps at each end, paved and with a chinaberry tree for shade, where a dog can have a nap, nursemaids can gossip while their charges romp, delivery boys can have a quick game of knucklebones, the kind of congenial little space that still keeps its Greek name, *plateia*, in Mediterranean languages (*place, plaza, piazza*). Here the mime would set up his business, perhaps with drum, fife, or lyre to collect an audience. He must depend on everybody's imagination to transform the air around him into a school, a room, a law court. He acts without a mask, but certainly with makeup. Some basic props serve him as he changes from character to character—hats, shawls, wigs, a walking stick. Mimicry is his art. The pleasure he gives is that of recognition of type. Once a human being has become fixed in his reactions and is predictable, he has become the matter of comedy.

Herondas is thus working in the tradition of Theophrastos and Menander. He has no political ground, like Aristophanes; no history or ideologies mingle with his art. New Comedy was portable anywhere and proved to be as native to Rome as Athens, to London and Madrid. It is the art of Jonson and Molière, of Waugh and Wodehouse. Herondas (as he seems to say in *The Dream*) considered himself to be reviving the satiric art of the poet Hipponax, who lived three centuries before him, and who can be bracketed with the master satirist Archilochos. It was the spirit of Hellenism to be retrospective, to restore and polish more vigorous art from previous times. Theokritos his contemporary, whose eclogues can be thought of as mimes (and may have been so performed in aristocratic households and at literary gatherings), and Kallimakhos, also his contemporary, were imitators of what they imagined to be a classical period, a golden age which they were reproducing in silver.

A play comes alive in performance only. Herondas would seem to admit of a wide range of interpretation by an actor. The stage directions which I have made up for this translation assume that these mimes were close to the art of Peter Sellers, of Zero Mostel, and Lily Tomlin—farces deliciously rendered by a master impersonator of types. It may well be, of course, that the acting was more savagely satiric—something close to the acid wit of the Goya of the *Caprichos*, one of which might illustrate *The Matchmaker*. Most of Herondas' interpreters, especially Will and Cunningham, see Herondas as a much darker figure than I do. I see no morbid overtones of sadism in *The Schoolmaster*, only an irate mother with a lout of a son to be disciplined. I can see nothing bawdy in *The Shoemaker*, only women trying on every shoe in a shop without buying any. I see nothing vilely obscene in *The Whorehouse Manager*, only a gloriously absurd plea by a half-literate businessman whose rhetoric is giving the judges a headache.

The very successful skits which the Roman actor Luigi Proietti has been doing in the last three years, called "A Me gli Occhi, Please," is probably a fairly close approximation of what Herondas' theatre was in Alexandria in the third century B.C. Proietti assumes one part after another. His props are all in a box—wigs, hats, coats—and his transformation from Calabrian farmer to blowhard politician to American country music singer are made before the audience. Playing without a mask, and without the traditional cloth phallus of the comic actor, Herondas' actor would have approached the realism of our time more closely than any other kind of theatre in antiquity. The recovery of his texts happened in the heyday of British pantomime, of the music halls with their turns and comic skits, of Marie Lloyd, practitioners of his very art. And when he was first translated in 1922, the mime was having a renaissance: the silent movies. Now, while the silent mime has masters like Marcel Marceau, and amateur mimes can be seen performing around the Beaubourg in Paris (the old stamping grounds of the Commedia dell' Arte in its day), and mimes are popular with theatrical groups everywhere, it is worthwhile attempting to make the first mimes to have survived from antiquity better known.

Headlam's translation of 1922 is into Edwardian diction and prose; the Knox translation of 1929 (Loeb Classics) is, in Cunningham's laconic judgment, "unhelpful." Louis Laloy's translation into French (Budé) lacks color and verve. Herondas' style is either antiqued (presumably to sound like his master Hipponax) or, as I would like to believe, solely on a hunch, in a particular Ionic vernacular, perhaps that of Kos. His words are tightly elided, his phrasing economic, always expressive, idiomatic, and frequently vulgar.

In his version of humanity in all its weakness we can recognize practically everything. It was a world that thought slaves comic in what it supposed to be their shiftlessness, a world that delighted to detect pretension, that charted every minim of movement outside one's social bounds. Battaros the whorehouse manager is comic because he is too stingy to hire a lawyer; it is also clear that he imagines himself to be as eloquent as any lawyer he could have hired. In all the mimes we see the characters as they cannot see themselves, and yet we understand very well how they think of themselves. Bitinna in *The Jealous Woman* sees herself as a generous woman sorely wronged; we see her as an indulgent woman who has spoiled her lover and has only herself to blame if he has an exaggerated notion of his charms. All of Herondas' characters are, in an old-fashioned and basic sense, fools. They stew in juices of their own brewing, and Herondas always leaves them there, between the art of the anecdote and that of the sketch, without the resolutions of comedy.

Imagine a *mimiambus* in which the actor does a cobbler of women's shoes, together with customers, in a comic moment that has remained a source of humor for 2,300 years.

It goes like this:[1]

(The actor wears a cobbler's smock over which he can put an ample stole to be his customer Metro, as hard-to-get-along-with a shopper as ever drove a shoe clerk to distraction. The women who have come with Metro can be indicated by gestures toward them, nudges, winks, and smirks.)

METRO
(Expansively, with middle-class condescension toward an inferior.)
Kerdon, I bring you these women friends here
To look at some of your beautiful work.

KERDON
(Overdoing it, as with all his fawning.)
No wonder, Metro, I'm your admirer!
(To a servant.)
Put the settle outside for these ladies.
(Nothing happens.)
It's you I mean, Drimylos. Are you deaf?
Asleep again!
(To another servant.)
Hit him on the nose, you!
Pistos! Kick the sleep out of that sad lout!
The behind! The neck! Twist both his arms off!
(To Drimylos.)
Up, you scoundrel! We can make it rougher.
(Seethes. More scandal.)
Dusting the bench, are you, at this late date?
Why, you white-assed punk, wasn't it kept clean?
I'll dust your seat, just you wait, with a plank.

[1]Cunningham and other commentators explain that this mime is really about women shopping for a *baubon*, or dildo. This error comes from a similarity of stock comic names. In Mime VI, Metro (Matron) and Kerdon (Fox) are customer and dealer respectively in the matter of a *baubon*. This playlet, however, is simply women looking at every pair of shoes in a shop, leaving without buying any: Blondie in the shoestore.

(To the women.)

Be seated, Metro, do.

(To a servant.)

That cabinet,[2]
Pistos, open it up. No, not that one,
The other one up there on the third shelf.
Bring us those beauties here. What luck, Metro!
What shoes you're going to see.

(To Pistos.)

Careful,
You pig, with that showcase.

(To the women.)

This shoe, Metro,
Perfectly shaped from various leathers,
Is a dandy. See, ladies, these firm soles,
These neat straps, the rounding off of the toe.
Nothing shoddy anywhere, all first rate.
Take the color, now—may Pallas answer
Your heart's prayer for the shoe of your dreams—
You won't find such color at the dyer's,
Nor yet such shine in an artist's beeswax.[3]
Cost three minas day before yesterday,
That pair did, from Kandas the wholesaler,
And a pair like them, I tell you the truth,
On my word, there is no point in lying,
I hope never to prosper in business
If he didn't say he was giving me
These items as a personal favor,
So to speak, what with the price of leather
Going up every day at the tanners.
A work of art's what you'll be buying,
Practically stealing it from my poor hands.
Night and day I wear out my bench working,
No time to eat, even, until sunset.
The din is worse than Mikion's wild beasts.[4]
Not to mention the thirteen slaves I need,

[2]The word may be simply *shoebox.*
[3]Greek painters mixed their colors in wax.
[4]A local zoo or menagerie?

Lazy dogs, the lot of them, they are too.
Business falls off a bit, and all you hear
Out of them is *Give me this, give me that.*
Business is brisk, they roost around like hens
Keeping their between the legs good and warm.
                    (Realizing that his digression isn't selling shoes.)
You can't spend promises on anything,
As they say: cash on the barrel for these,
Or for as good a pair, we have lots more.
We'll keep showing until you're pleased.
Bring out all the cabinets here, Pistos.
What a pity if you don't find a pair.
But you will. Look here. There is every style:
Sikonian and Ambrakidian,
Nossises, Khian, parrots and hemp soles,
Saffron mules and around the house slippers,
Ionian button tops and night walkers,
High ankles, crab claws, Argeian sandals,
Cockscombs, cadets, flat heels. Just tell me now.
Ladies, what's your heart's desire. Speak right out.
Women and dogs, as we all know, eat shoes.[5]

METRO

How much are you asking for that first pair?
And don't talk such a storm, you'll drive us
Out of your shop with all this jabbering.

KERDON

(Unfazed, inured to nattering women.)
Price it yourself, dear madam, whatever
You think is just, or this pair, or this.
What's fairer than that? How could I cheat you
If I let you set the value yourself?
If you know true work, make me an offer.
May a fox make its den in my grey hair,
My hair grey as ashes, if I don't sell you
Fine shoes today and eat well tomorrow.

---

[5]Cunningham has a long note here on shoe fetishism, which he tries to tie in with his conviction that the shoes are not shoes but dildos. The proverb would seem to be transparent: dogs chew on shoes and women wear them out and buy them with frantic regularity. Human nature is constant; Greek women of the Alexandrian period doubtless owned, as women now, fifteen to every one pair of shoes belonging to their husbands.

*(Aside, to the audience, hamming his lines like
a traditional villain, rubbing his greedy hands.)*

Hermes the Fox and Peitho the Vixen!
I shall haul something in for supper
With this cast of the net, or know why not!

METRO

Why do you mutter and ramble on so
And not give the price with an honest tongue?

KERDON

Look high, look low, this pair is a mina.
Ladies, if you were Pallas Athena
The price would be the same, not a cent less.

METRO

(Her patience gone, fire in her eye.)

I see now why your cabinets are full,
Kerdon. Works of art, indeed, that you keep
For yourself, clearly not for customers.

(Archly.)

The twentieth of Taureon, you know,
Is Hekatê's daughter Artakenê's
Wedding, for which new shoes will be needed.
They will all come here, I am sure they will,
So you'd better get a sack for a purse
For what they'll spend, and you can dread thieves.

KERDON

(Unimpressed.)

For Hekatê as for Artakenê
The price is still a mina, be assured,
As it is for you, when you make your choice.

METRO

(With practiced sarcasm.)

Is it not your luck, Kerdon, to touch
Charming feet which love and desire have touched,
And you the scab off of a running sore?

*(Looks around among her friends, pleased with herself, for having put this
scum of a merchant in his place. Moves in on Kerdon for the kill.)*

Now you can, you think, manipulate me,
But not my friend here. What will you charge her
For that pair? Think again before you speak.

KERDON
(Undaunted, brassy as ever.)
Five staters, by the gods, are offered me
Daily by Eveteris the psaltrist
For that pair, but I wouldn't sell them to her
If she were to make the price four darics.
She flits around making fun of my wife
And she can go barefoot for all I care.
(Changing tactics while he has the upper hand.)
If you indeed want them, take these three pairs,
But for nothing less than seven darics.
I couldn't dream of it. Seven darics.
(Leaps to fill the vacuum of their hesitation.)
How could I deny you, Metro, anything?
(Smiling foxily.)
You, Metro, whose voice lifts me to the gods,
A shoemaker, a very stone, you lift.
(Imagines he is quoting from poetical speeches he has heard at the theatre.)
For your tongue is not a tongue but a whisk
For delights. Like one of the gods is he,
Ah! who hears you talking day in day out!
(Squats, a shoe in his hand.)
Stick your tiny foot out now and let me
Slip this shoe on it.
(Throws up hands in wonderment.)
Fits to perfection!
What possible improvement could you want?
(Quotes again, finger beside nose.)
Beautiful things belong to the beautiful!
You would think that Athena made this shoe.
(Quickly, to another woman.)
You, if you please, your foot.
(Removes her shoe and holds it up for all to see.)
What! Did an ox
Make you this shoe, imitating its hoof?
(Fits on one of his shoes.)
If my knife had followed your foot's outline,
Could the fit of this shoe have been nicer?
By my household altar, it's perfect!

(To another woman, who is already leaving.)
You at the door snickering like a horse
At me and my wares, seven darics now,
And this pair is all yours, what do you say?
*(The women are all gathering themselves to leave,
having seen every shoe in the place.)*
Well, you need sandals for around the house.
Or bedroom slippers. So just send a slave.
(On a hopeful note.)
Remember, Metro, red shoes by the ninth,
In good time for the wedding, keep in mind.
(Proverbially.)
Winter clothes must be made in summer heat.
(Looks heavenward in disgust.)

Ariadne's Dancing Floor

Joyce worked the texture of each of his books with a more complex intricacy of symbol and allusion than the one before. We have begun to see, through a wealth of critical studies, how he achieved this richness of text by concealing figures in a mazelike ground of such cunning entanglement that they have to be discovered. *Riddle*, Joyce never lets us forget, is the frequentive of *read*. Without daring to pose a unified theory of Joyce's symbolic structures, I am going to consider this richness of his text as an aesthetic ideal which involved all of his formal concerns and which, moreover, is the distinguishing characteristic of twentieth-century art.

The imaginative bonding of images in an harmonic pattern would seem to be the naked principle of Joyce's method. This is the method of all art, and one artist differs from another in the quality of invention with which he bonds one image to another. All of Joyce's books fit together as a unity, an *oeuvre*. The archaic Greek mind ascribed all things cunningly wrought, whether a belt with a busy design, the rigging of a ship, or an extensive palace, to the art of the craftsman Daedalus, whose name first appears in the *Iliad*. Homer, describing the shield Hephaistos makes for Akhilleus, says that the dancing floor depicted on it was as elaborate as that which Daedalus designed for Ariadne in Crete. This dancing floor is perhaps what Homer understood the Labyrinth to be. Joyce did, for the ground on which he places all his figures is clearly meant to be a labyrinth. Such floors, usually in mosaic, persist through history, spread by Graeco-Roman culture, and can be found in cathedrals (Bayeux and Chartres, for example), villas, city plans, squares, and formal gardens. They all display an interlacing of lines in a pattern that doubles back on itself in a "commodus vicus of recirculation" as a cicerone's voice says in the opening paragraph of *Finnegans Wake*, which is a small model of a labyrinth containing other Joycean images of the kind of mazes he will elaborate on (and has elaborated on in all his previous books): rivers, time as shaped by history and myth, and choice environs (a word that derives from the Latin for the twistings and turnings of streets in a city).

A page of the *Wake* is meant, as we know from the text itself (FW 122.23), to resemble the convoluted strapwork of the illuminated pages of the Book of Kells. Three traditions flow together to make the style of these pages: the uncial upper-and-lower-case mode of writing the Latin alphabet from which all modern Western typefaces derive, a fanciful and punning employment of animals as decorative detail inherited from barbaric and prehistoric art, and interlaced strapwork copied from the mosaic floors of Roman buildings, which descend in direct tradition from that dancing floor of Ariadne's in Crete attributed by Homer to Daedalus.

It is usual for mediaeval strapwork to make a continuum, to wind through many swerves and bends, and end where it began, frequently tied in a rich Celtic knot, or nipped in a beak. Such a decorative line loops through all of Joyce's prose narratives. The first word of *Dubliners*, *there*, knits in with the last word of the *Wake*, *the*, which we are to understand as continuing on to the first word of the *Wake*, *riverrun*, making the text circular. We can now recognize the linking word *theriver*, the Dublin pronunciation of *therever*, an adverb compounded of a word indicating space and a word indicating time, the two great tonal symbols of the *Wake*, a kind of cosmic knot Joyce ties in his subject matter at the end of episodes, usually by summoning the presence of the theoretician of time and space as aspects of each other, Einstein, who, as elm (he was born at *Ulm*, Elm) and stone, organic and inorganic matter, turns out to be Shem and Shaun and all the other dualities in the book which by opposing each other, cooperate.

There are other ways of looking at the endless end and beginningless beginning of the *Wake*. One of the prototypes of the *Wake* is the Egyptian Book of the Dead. *Riverrun*, a coined word, is based on the French *riverain*, "riverside," a quotation from Napoleon's will (asking that he be buried near the banks of the Seine, as he is, in the Invalides church, beside a museum of his era, a tour of which occupies pages 8–10 of the *Wake*), but is also a translation of the Egyptian hieroglyph (two horizontal and parallel wavy lines) meaning *to flow*, or *river*. If we append the appropriate definite article, we have a duck in flight, and if we take this article to be the translation of the *the* at the end of the *Wake*, we have found Joyce's cunning rhyme with the end of *Ulysses*, the *yes* of Penelope-Molly (*penelops*, a duck).

That *yes* is itself a loop-back to the first word of *Ulysses*, *stately*, in which its letters are distributed backwards. Removed, as if for use as the last word of the book, the remainder is *tat*, to be seen as a Kells decoration, an *alpha* (for Christ, who at Rev. 21:6 gives that as a symbol for Himself) between two crosses: the crucifixion. And an *l*, or *El*, God the Father. There is more. Joyce wants his beginning words to be convoluted mediaeval capitals which on imaginative inspection are as richly entwined as the capital letters in the Book of Kells. *Stately* and *plump* fit into the series of symbols in the first chapter which identify Stephen as Everyman in the clutches of Riot, missing his inheritance, as Prince Hal under the sway of Falstaff, a melancholy prince in an inversion of degree, subjugated by a peasant (the 1882 Skeat's *Concise Etymological Dictionary* that the young Joyce carried in his pocket derives *plump* from ME *plomp*, "rude, clownish"). We can also divide *stately* into *tat*, the crucifixion, the Greek word for nature, ῬΥΛΗ, and an S, which in this series of symbols (Creation, Fall, and Redemption) would be the snake in Eden. In fact, we are prompted to do so by the sandwich-board men who bear each a letter of Wisdom Hely's ambulant ad, not always in orthographic order, and with S lagging behind. *Stately* was a very carefully chosen word.

Dubliners begins with the word *there*, and ends with *dead*; *A Portrait* with *once* and *stead*; *Ulysses*, *stately* and *yes*; *Finnegans Wake*, *riverrun* and *the*, with the two fusing into *theriver*. The fusion also serves to keep the vowel [ɛ] constant in all the end words.

Figures in mediaeval art often occupy contours that delineate other shapes, making a visual pun. The ambivalent images may be simple and obvious, such as a fish with a curved tail for the letter J, or complex and typological, such as an Orpheus charming the animals which can also be read as Noah filling the ark. Images which can be seen as more than one thing occur in the most archaic art, in the cave drawings of Aurignacian times, in primitive art the world over. Shields and masks from New Guinea show a second face when inverted. Joyce owned Freud's study of Leonardo, *Eine Kindheitserinnerung des Leonardo da Vinci* (1910), at the time he was writing *A Portrait*, and may have seen in it strategies for shaping the complex multiple symbolism of the bird-girl epiphany in Chapter IV. Freud's study attempts to connect a dream of Leonardo's and the outline of a vulture which can be seen as a visual pun in Leonardo's *The Virgin and St. Anne*. Freud's scholarship is cockeyed (he mistook Dmitri Merejkowski's *The Romance of Leo-*

nardo da Vinci, a fictional life, for a biography, mistranslated *nibbio* (*kite*) as *vulture*, and concocted a fantasy as dreamlike as the one he supposed he was analyzing with scientific nicety). Joyce was aware of this forgery of Freud-as-Shem-the-Penman: in the *Wake*, page 300, we can find in the maze "nibbleh ravensostonnoriously ihs mum to me in bewonderment" wherein we can see the *nibbio* in conjunction with a madonna and child ("ihs mum"). And in a footnote one Dav Stephens (da Vinci and Stephen Dedalus inside the one contour), who, we can learn from Adaline Glasheen's *Third Census*, was Davy Stephens, a Dublin eccentric and newspaper seller who liked to dress up as a gentleman for Derby Day.

We can, however, understand that Joyce saw in Freud's study an instigation for shaping symbols with multiple contents inside a single outline. The bird-girl must primarily be a dancer on Ariadne's dancing floor, for it was a crane-dance that was performed there. Secondly she must be a symbol of Stephen's soul, for there is an ancient and widespread symbolism in mythology and folklore of a bird as the soul.

The image of the bird-girl unfolds like the progressions of a metamorphosis in Ovid. It begins to take shape in the director's condescending banter about the awkwardness of the Belgian capuchins' garb rucked out in an ungainly fashion, like skirts (*jupes*) while riding bicycles. The image is next developed when Stephen sees a "faded blue shrine of the Blessed Virgin which stood fowlwise on a pole in the middle of a hamshaped encampment of poor cottages." The director had unknowingly put his foot in it when he chose to criticize the capuchins, for it was a capuchin to whom Stephen had confessed after his waywardness. It is as if two lines of force cross each other in this crucial scene, and they are not lines; they are circles. There is a complex symbolism of circles in this chapter, turning up in the bicycle wheels of the Belgian capuchin, in the moon, everywhere if you are alert to them, and culminating in the hoop buried in the sand at the end of the chapter, symbolizing the soul's cycle from God and back again, a segment of its circumference passing through matter just as the hoop on the beach is partly imbedded in sand.

Stephen has a choice of cycles: the life of a priest, the life of an artist. He had been on the right cycle for the artist in his sinful binge (Joyce seeing that sexual energy is the first inchoate and undirected energy of the creative spirit). What the director is proposing, from the fledgling artist's perspective, is to negate and paralyze that energy. Stephen intuitively moves over to the alternate cycle, the way of the artist, and is vouchsafed his vision.

He confirms the vision in the *Wake* by returning it to the midden of ancient imagery from which it arose. On St. Stephen's Day all over Europe it is customary to kill a bird and display it on a pole. In Ireland the bird is a wren. In "The Ballad of Persse O'Reilly" (FW 44–47) we keep hearing "the rann, the king of all ranns," which is "the wren, the king of all birds" of the boys' song on St. Stephen's Day + *rann*, Gaelic for refrain + Ran, the Norse sea-goddess Rán, whose locale was inlets and pools by the seaside.

Eighteen months after the publication of *Finnegans Wake*, when Joyce and his family were among the millions of refugees plunged into flight across Europe by the German armies, five children from Montignac in the Val Dordogne discovered the prehistoric cave Lascaux with its painted animals and signs, the first flowering of European art. Among the figures in this cave is a bird on a pole, the remotest ancestor of Joyce's symbol. The ritual of hunting wrens on St. Stephen's Day in Ireland probably has affinities (of thirty thousand years' continuity) with the hieratic bird painted with elk fat and charcoal in Lascaux. There is a sense in which Lascaux is part of the texture of the *Wake*: Joyce had prepared our sensibilities for seeing Lascaux. Lascaux is very much a part of our reading Joyce.

Such fortuity has always been a problem for scholars. How much has Joyce worked into his text? Where do we stop? Was Joyce aware of Paul Chabas' painting *September Morn* when he constructed his bird-girl in the *Portrait*? He probably wasn't, yet there it is, a vernacular statement of his symbol. He had the kind of mind that would have appreciated this vulgate parallel, a version of Stephen's vision for Bloom to go with Gerty MacDowell, "a seaside girl," who moreover shared the dock with *Ulysses* in New York when the Society for the Suppression of Vice hauled them both into court.

Reading Joyce one is always going to encounter puzzling knots in his Daedalian twists and turns. Joyce seeded some of his symbols, apparently at random, like mitochondria with their separate DNA and RNA inside cells already well supplied with genetic codes. They are as yet unaccountable, and may be illusions. In Chapter IV of the *Portrait*, for example, there are scattered puns and images that seem to come from Carlo Collodi's *Pinocchio*, a book Joyce owned at the time. Stephen eats slim jim from a cricket cap while "Some jesuits were walking round the cycletrack in the company of ladies." We recognize the circle symbol that persists throughout this chapter, and can connect it with Stephen's choice between circle and tangent, obedience to or rebellion from order, priest and artist.

Pinocchio is a child's book about a talking and autokinetic puppet who is seduced away from his kindly artisan father (Joyce would have seen Daedalus and Ikaros in the pair) by evil companions (Lucignolo is one, a fox another, perhaps Joyce's "face of one of the jesuits whom some of the boys called Lantern Jaws and others Foxy Campbell") against the advice of Pinocchio's conscience, a cricket. Thinking that he is going to a boy's paradise of candy trees and lemonade rivers, he is actually going to be changed into a donkey working a mill ("cycletrack"). He escapes, and his metamorphosis into a human boy is presided over by a Buona Fata. If one is looking for a synthesis of folktales as a deep substratum in popular literature for the *Portrait*, Collodi will answer.

But what kind of game is Joyce playing with that "slim jim out of a cricketcap"? *Slim jim* (sticks of jerked beef, a schoolboy delicacy) is an obvious signature of the kind Joyce can be discovered tucking into his text, and it is likely that Slim Jim was an inevitable nickname in his adolescence. *Jiminy Cricket* is an age-old euphemism; the OED gives early nineteenth-century examples. Joyce has linked *jim* and *cricket*, cycletrack and Collodi's donkey-powered mill. It is as if Joyce recognized an elective affinity among images, however metaphysically witty, and hoped they would bond together in a kind of poetic chemistry. Whether the reader is missing something by not finding these recondite allusions is like asking if one can fully appreciate Chartres while being ignorant of its engineering, its history, and the iconography of all its sculpture. Ultimately, as with Chartres, we realize that Joyce wrote with a faith in his materials and his method that lies beyond even extraordinary study. Like Proust, he compared his work to cathedral building: a grandeur of thrust and presence, and a painstaking care in the significance of the minutest details.

Another example. In the first section of the Wandering Rocks chapter of *Ulysses*, which traces a perambulation of a priest along the streets of Dublin, we read:

> On Newcomen bridge the very reverend John Conmee S. J. of saint Francis Xavier's church, upper Gardiner street, stepped on to an outward bound tram.
> Off an inward bound tram stepped the reverend Nicholas Dudley C. C. of saint Agatha's church, north William street, on to Newcomen bridge.
> At Newcomen bridge Father Conmee stepped into an outward bound tram for he disliked to traverse on foot the dingy way past Mud Island.

Several strands of the symbolic web crisscross here. Throughout this chapter people and things (including narrative style and grammar, as Clive Hart has shown in a brilliant essay)[1] seem to collide, but don't, and seem to con-

[1]"Wandering Rocks," in *James Joyce's* Ulysses: *Critical Essays*, edited by Clive Hart and David Hayman (Berkeley and Los Angeles: University of California Press, 1974), 181–216.

figure: they come together, like Homer's Symplegades, only to part. The passing of the two priests here would be meaningful in Dickens or a detective novel. Joyce is playing a game with our attention. The bridge is named Newcomen. These sentences seesaw like the beam of a Newcomen steam engine. Does the Rev. Dudley get his name from the fact that the first Newcomen engine was built at Dudley Castle, Staffordshire? The bonding of names would seem here to be footling and trivial. Does St. Agatha, patron of bell founders, interact with the great missionary St. Francis Xavier? St. Francis is there to disgrace and satirize Father Conmee's shallow and smug meditations on the salvation of savages. Is St. Agatha there to match the swaying of bells with the swaying of the beam of a Newcomen engine: another image of things that seem to collide, the Age of Faith and the Age of Machines? And priests and bridges (*pons, pontifex*), and Nicholas and John (the saints with those names open vistas of symbolic interpretation), and are we to remember that we are near the site of "An Encounter" and thus see things Bunyanesque in Mud Island?

What is the relationship between figure and ground? It is characteristic of modern (as of mediaeval) art that figure and ground interpenetrate. We can explain cubism by noting that Picasso and Braque developed Cézanne so that figure is subsumed by ground. In a pun, figure and ground can change place with each other, as in the pointillist charts for determining color blindness. Like Arcimboldo, Tchelitchew, and Freud's da Vinci, Joyce habitually reworks his ground and renders it figure.

In the mimicry of styles in The Oxen of the Sun we see a continuous figure evolve, in imitation of the foetus developing from fecundation to birth. The ground, however, on which this figure moves is yet another labyrinth, like the corridors of schools and streets of Dublin and Cork in the *Portrait*, and the effect is that of a voice in time, assuming the sensibilities, outlook, and limitations of the perspective peculiar to age after age, but always within the genus of voice in which Joyce is a kinsman, taking now this turn that Sir Thomas Browne would have taken, now that native to Smollett, or Dickens, or Carlyle. Style, as in all of *Ulysses*, is here identified with fate. What and how we see is determined by the quality of our attention. Theseus in the turns of the labyrinth was looking for a monster with whom he must fight to the death, Ariadne's thread in one hand, sword in the other. All else was absent from his heroic ecstasy of purpose.

Bloom, Stephen, and Molly, treaders of labyrinths of rooms, furniture, streets, and memory (every chapter of *Ulysses* is its own kind of labyrinth), have no such purpose, though Joyce by bonding figure and ground in a harmony of symbols assigns them a purpose, a fate discernible in signs.

It was Giambattista Vico's theory that archaic families of signs survive in words. These aboriginal meanings are like prehistoric objects recoverable from middens, like the Dead Sea Scrolls, weapons, kitchen utensils, figurines of goddesses. Joyce wrote all his books as palimpsests *over* objects in this midden, and eventually over his own work. *Ulysses* is written over a specific text; the *Wake* is written over the tattered, fused, living web of spoken language. We hear this rush of sounds with an ear that hears English best in the polyglot babble and usually makes English sense of everything heard, no matter what language it is.

The polyphonic closing page of the *Wake* recapitulates *Chamber Music*. This suite of thirty-six lyrics in the Elizabethan mode is a progression following the seasons of the year, a love affair that ends in grief, and the course of a river from its source to the sea. Like *Dubliners* it ends with an image of mutinous, plunging waves. All of Joyce's works culminate in a diffusion of spirit that is both an annihilation and a union. By linking his last work to his first, he insists that his books are an *oeuvre* in a structure of great unity and symmetry. Each work follows and absorbs the preceding. The *Wake* is a night complementing the day of *Ulysses*. Both the *Portrait* and *Ulysses* are derived from *Dubliners*, as many critical studies have demonstrated. Perhaps we can say that all Joyce's themes resolve into one: the encounter of the unique, innocent soul with a world stained by guilt, defeat, and delusion.

Once we have plotted the ways of Joyce's labyrinthine symbolism, will we possess a vision, some ineffable wisdom? No. For Joyce's symbolism is a mimesis of symbolism: a dramatic perception, ultimately tragic, that man's ideas, his art, his noblest configurations of sense, are no more than symbols. They are forgeries of meaning. Their only validity inheres in their being a system, or family, one thing kin to another in a way that we will probably never understand. The systems cohere and function, and have the inviolable integrity of languages.

Joyce builds within a strong frame. If time is a river, matter is its bed, motionless in relation to time's flow. The river runs into the sea, losing its identity and form. But evaporation from its surface and from trees and grass it has nourished, rises to make rain, which falls on the Wicklow hills and becomes the river again.

Humanity evaporates moment by moment in voices which ring against ears. We participate in the self-renewing cycles of nature, but language is our own continuum. At the very root of all Joyce's styles is the wondering appreciation that there must be all over the world phrases, rhythms of speech, and ideas that are older than any other trace of man's past. Joyce's faith was that these midden meanings are not lost but sleeping, and that the most daring challenge of the artist was to grasp the reality of this fabric of the imagination.

Ulysses is what this communal myth looks like seen from the Mediterranean, in cross section and on a single day. Modern Europe is in one sense a transposition of Mediterranean culture. *Ulysses*, like the *Wake*, begins in a bay to which Mediterranean culture can come, and ends at Gibraltar, the beginning of the route. The *Wake*, in turn, is Europe seen from the north, from Scandinavia, from the forests. Each work is *catholic* in a different sense. In *Ulysses* the whole world (*katholikos*) derives from a field of forces the poles of which are Jerusalem and Rome, Bible and Odyssey, sacred and civil. The *Wake* explores the archaic foretime that gave birth to Jerusalem and Rome, and traces history in the reverberations from centers of power rather than the centers themselves. Its basic tale is of every achieved harmony invaded and wrecked: Eden by Satan, the first family by Cain's violence, the scriptorium at Kells by Danish marauders. We rise, we fall. We may rise by falling. Defeat shapes us. Our only wisdom is tragic, known too late, and only to the lost.

Joyce's achievement is to have fulfilled in a masterly *oeuvre* a particular promise of art in the twentieth century. We can define elements of his mastery by placing him beside his peers. Pound, so curiously hostile to the *Wake* and eventually disenchanted with *Ulysses* after he had championed it, was working parallel to Joyce in that he was tracking the beginnings of civilizations and cultures, and meditating on what qualities made them vulnerable to destruction or guaranteed them long life. But whereas Pound hoped to instruct mankind and display history as a lesson, Joyce did not. Man is tragically man, never to elude his fate.

Thomas Mann and Proust both attempted an inclusive and exhaustive configuration of European society, and both built complex symbolic structures which can be compared with Joyce's. Mann beside Joyce appears pedantic, mechanical, humorless. The life that Joyce breathed into his work is not there. Beside Mann, Joyce's success at integrating all the elements of his work into a moving, articulate whole becomes clear. Mann imposes meaning; Joyce finds it; Mann looks for weakness in strength; Joyce, for strength in weakness. Mann's novels illustrate ideas; Joyce's return ideas to their origins.

Proust, so distant from Joyce in temperament and method, is yet strangely close to him in saturating an exact realism with a pervasive internal symbolism. A set of affinities exists between Joyce's water nymphs (from the *Portrait* to ALP) and Proust's frieze of girls against the sea at Balbec, between Bloom and Swann, Molly and Odette. Their delineations of the childhood of Stephen Dedalus and little Marcel define two cultures, and their studies of the provincialism of Dublin and of the Faubourgs St.-Honoré and St.-Germain are the two classics of their genre. How time deepens and forces tragedy is a common theme. They bear strongest resemblance, surprisingly, in their coming to accept the reader as a presence felt in the act of composition. When the novel arises, it is in front of a congenial and friendly audience. The narrator of *Don Quixote* tells his audience straightway that he isn't certain of his hero's name (as if we might be able to supply it), and authors throughout the eighteenth century are variously diplomatic, polite, and confiding to an assumed civilized reader. This congeniality ends after, perhaps with, Dickens and Scott, both of whom have designs on the reader's morals and sensibilities. The novelist becomes a teacher, the reader a pupil. Realism banishes the reader altogether. Flaubert gives the impression that he would have written his novels if he were alone in the world. As alienation becomes a major theme, the greatest alienation is that of the reader. For whom did Kafka write his stories? What audience did Pound have in mind for *The Cantos*? There is heroism here (witness Picasso and cubism, Ives and his audienceless, unplayed music, Gertrude Stein and her Olympian disdain for readers), as there is arrogance, sometimes justifiable, sometimes unforgivable.

It would seem that the text of *Finnegans Wake* and Proust's 2,265 pages of digressions spawning digressions are ultimate examples of the writer estranged from and unaware of any reader whatever. They are the opposite: both reestablish an intimate friendship with readers. Proust treats his audience as a member of his circle, discusses his characters with him, begs for patience, and in the end explains that to hear him out is not to ingest his story but to be made aware of ours. His novel, he says, is an optical instrument with which the reader sees himself.

Joyce in the *Wake* dispenses with the godlike method he used to write all his books through *Ulysses*. The text is a game, often a comic riddle of outrageous fun and ingenuity. We are repeatedly urged to read the text aloud. A wonderful buffoonery and wickedly accurate mimicry is in full spiel; whatever the joke is, it is decidedly a joke and not a book at all for the audience that sits respectful before Mann, in awe of his learning, irony, and philosophical subtlety; not a book for Zola's earnest readers; not a book you would expect in our century at all. Sit down with the most melancholy and lyric evocation of the past in our time, Hermann Broch's Brucknerish *Death of Virgil,* and then turn to the *Wake.* The transition is like turning from an erudite string quartet to an Elizabethan street fair.

We have yet, after all these years, to admit that the *Wake* belongs to the art of the mime, to the most vulgar and riotous of the arts. True, it is a text of the most demanding sense, the most exacting of all his works. But it is cast in the mode of the most primitive of European art forms, the communal party, drunken, obscene, orgiastic, loud with singing, rich in license: the kermis, the wedding frolic, the Irish funeral, the ritual dances on Ariadne's patterned floor. The circle is immense that Joyce bent back to its origin: from a bleak story about a priest who dropped a chalice, a death, and a dreary wake, to a summoning of that chalice in all its permutations sacred and profane, to a drunken gathering of the human family, where the old tales are told over again, and where the decorum is, beyond all sense, to grieve and rejoice to-gether.

The Smith of Smiths

Though he is given fifty-two entries in *The Oxford Dictionary of Quotations* (twenty-eight more than Mark Twain) and all of us quote him unknowingly ("square peg in a round hole"), we have to be reminded who the Reverend Sydney Smith was. Unlike Doctor Johnson, he had no Boswell. Nor in his *Collected Works* (five volumes of sermons, essays, and political and ecclesiastical pamphlets) is there a single text that one might reprint as evidence of Smith's abilities as an author.

Sydney Smith belongs to the history of British liberalism and reform, to the history of the Church of England, to the history of London society, and to the history—when someone compiles it—of conversation. He entered the church with no great religious fervor; his family had educated him at Winchester and New College, Oxford, and the church was a living for a man with civilized and scholarly tastes. And though he advanced slowly in ecclesiastical preferment, ending his days as canon of Saint Paul's, the church gave him a context for his love of people.

Smith's father was a curmudgeon, a tyrant, and a man of incredible meanness; he lived to bedevil his sons until he was ninety. The parson, who married a woman as good-natured as he was, seems to have wanted to be wholly unlike his terrible father, and to create around himself a world of benevolence and good will—the opposite of his jaundiced father's cinder heap of a world.

Sydney Smith was, quite simply, a good man, an example of abundant good nature. His was an age when clergymen could cure souls they had never laid eyes on. He tried this route as a young man, finagling a comfortable post in London while drawing pay from a distant and invisible congregation. This abuse was coming under criticism about the time he was settling in to exploit it. He was one of the first of the clergy to reform and move to his parish.

This he did with good grace, though it was to the wilds of Yorkshire. And it was here, after having founded the *Edinburgh Review* and penetrated into the heart of British society and politics—as a fixture at Holland House, a popular London lecturer, a skillful pamphleteer for the Whigs—that Sydney Smith became Sydney Smith. The parish had had no resident clergyman for 150 years. When, in his first sermon, Smith struck a cushion for emphasis, the dust that flew out obscured his view of the congregation.

Here at Foston Parsonage (which he designed and built; it still stands, a charming place), he undertook to be a shepherd to his flock, gentry and farmers together. He introduced the kitchen garden to balance farm diets, consulted agronomists to improve crops and labor, and worked a model farm of his own. He refused to hunt the fox, as an unchristian act. There was no doctor in the community, so he took an elementary medical course, set up a pharmacy, and doctored man and beast without pay. He plied the stomach pump and scalpel, delivered babies, and set limbs. Of a desperately sick infant he wrote, "I first gave it a dose of castor-oil and then I christened it; so now the poor child is ready for either world."

It was while he was at Foston that Smith risked his reputation to defend Catholic emancipation. He risked it even further in criticizing Baptists and Methodists for their ranting and narrow-mindedness. All his life he was willing to fight for tolerance, reform, and fairness. His home was an island of civilization, and as wonderfully eccentric as England could boast. He had a female butler. He insisted that his servants be independent minded. He could not bear subservience, and treated his household staff as dignified people holding jobs in a friendly family.

Smith is a fine example of the kind of man who can make the best of anything. At his first miserable parsonage near Salisbury, his very first encounter with Christian realities was finding clothes for poor children so that they would not have to come to church naked. A man less spiritually gifted might well have turned away from the church altogether; Smith chose to learn how to communicate with the poor and how to alleviate poverty.

He escaped this parish by becoming a private tutor and chaplain to an aristocrat's sons. The French Revolution squashed his plans to take them to the continent. He took them to Edinburgh instead, where he met the intellectuals with whom he founded the *Edinburgh Review*, and where his delicious sense of humor was whetted into an instrument that still holds up as one of the sharpest tongues in the history of wit.

British humor is at its best with the ridiculous, and Smith was a master of glorious nonsense. When the *Review*'s editor Francis Jeffrey was plagued by supporters of an Arctic expedition, he refused to cooperate and shocked one of them by damning the North Pole. This was reported indignantly to Smith, who replied, "Never mind Jeffrey. Why, I have heard him speak disrespectfully of the Equator." He said of a man that "he deserved to be preached to death by wild curates." When a wooden pavement was being considered around Saint Paul's, he remarked, "Let the dean and Canons lay their heads together and the thing will be done."

He could sound like Wilde: "I never read a book before reviewing it; it prejudices a man so." Like Voltaire: "Minorities are almost always in the right." Like Johnson: "It requires a surgical operation to get a joke well into a Scotch understanding." Like Sam Butler: "Not body enough to cover his mind decently with; his intellect is improperly exposed." Like Diogenes: "I never could find a man who could think for two minutes together."

These *mots* were passed around from the Regency to early Victorian times. Then the coarseness and bite of some of them fell out of favor; Smith's robust mixture of practical Christianity, fun, and brave plain-speaking ran afoul of the new seriousness, piety, and habit of thinking theoretically rather than with common sense.

In fact, when Smith died in 1845, he was dangerously close to entering a time into which he would not fit. He had read each of Scott's novels as they came from the press, and was an admirer of Dickens. He had welcomed the train, and had even, just before he died, brought about a change in the way it was run. It was common practice to lock passengers in, for safety. This also trapped them in case of an accident, and was not the Smith way of doing things at all. A few pamphlets and some brilliant letters to the *Times* got the doors unlocked.

This was the way Smith had always done things. His *Peter Plymley's Letters* cajoled and shamed Parliament and the church into Catholic emancipation. He knew how to get around people and how to get between their ribs. He will never be sainted (in a sane world he could be the saint of Practical and Calm Solutions); he was not a thinker; literature can't quite claim him. He frequently stepped on toes, never on feelings. He is simply there, a good man in his time, an example.

Of course there are his letters; two volumes were published by the Clarendon Press in 1953, edited by Nowell Charles Smith. And after an extensive search, Alan Bell, an archivist at the National Library of Scotland, has turned up enough letters for two more volumes. Bell's biography,[1] which gives us a clearer and better-detailed view of Smith than was formerly possible, is based on these thousands of newly collected letters.

Bell's edition of a thousand more of Smith's letters, to add to the thousand we already have, will be a welcome event, for Smith was as delightful on paper as at dinner at Holland House or at Breakfast Rogers' breakfasts. And it is to be hoped that this rich, sharply concise biography will restore Smith to our sense of his time, and of his purpose. He is far more useful to study than the monsters and rascals who dirty the pages of history books.

One glimpse of the man as you can see him over and over in this biography, to whet your curiosity. Once at Combe Florey in Somerset, he hung oranges in the trees, for the beauty of it, and fitted his donkeys with felt antlers, for the joke of it, and herded them under his orange-bearing cedars, and invited the neighborhood in for cider and fruitcake, for the fun of it.

[1] Alan Bell, *Sydney Smith* (Oxford: Oxford University Press, 1980).

The Artist as Critic

"When he claims to be solitary," Claude Lévi-Strauss says in *The Way of the Masks*, "the artist lulls himself in a perhaps fruitful illusion, but the privilege he grants himself is not real. When he thinks he is expressing himself spontaneously, creating an original work, he is answering other past or present, actual or potential creators. Whether one knows it or not, one never walks alone along the path of creativity."

A glance at any shelf of literary studies will ascertain that we pay attention to the genesis of a work of art, whether Shakespeare's source material, where Ezra Pound got all the images built into *The Cantos*, what Joyce read, what stimuli were agitating the nerves of Marcel Proust. We do this with some faith that if we know origins we have a clue to ends and purposes. What we mainly learn, however, is that the sources of a work of art are in one sense negligible—that an inert block of marble became the *Moses* of Michelangelo, that a humble pamphlet about a highwayman became an intriguing text by Defoe, and then the *Jonathan Wild* of Henry Fielding, and generated energies that gave us *The Beggar's Opera* and Brecht's *Dreigroschen Oper*. An even humbler pamphlet begat Melville's *Israel Potter*.

We would like to learn other things from studying the gestation of a work of art, and this wish usually occurs just when we are suspicious that we are going in the wrong direction. Santayana gives us this warning: "To understand how the artist felt, however, is not criticism; criticism is an investigation of what the work is good for."

How naively do we expect a study of sources to help us understand a novel or painting or poem? Nineteenth-century biographers habitually calculated the genetic composition of their subjects. How much Scots blood plus how much Celtic blood; this to explain a level and logical head with a dash of superstition and imagination. Thomas Mann wrote all his books as if he indeed believed that he was a genius fabricated from a Baltic Lutheran German practical father (hence method, hard work, ambition) and a Portuguese Jewish warm emotional mother (from whom his sensuality, feeling, sympathy, love of beauty). This is, of course, myth, but a pervasive one. Joyce believed it, and sustained a tension between the Mediterranean and the North Sea; Keats believed it; art historians believe it, and explain Renaissance painting as a marriage of northern technique and Italian sentiment.

Lévi-Strauss says that it is a fruitful illusion in which the artist lulls himself when he claims to be solitary. And that the reality of the matter is that he is answering other creators. This answering can be quite conscious, as when Fielding parodies Richardson, or when Keats answers a sonnet with a sonnet in the matter of the color blue. Does not the novel begin with Cervantes answering a question Boiardo and Ariosto did not know they had asked? Response is a classical tactic of all art. Brancusi's *The Kiss*, which seems to be two boxes embracing, is a response to Rodin's romantic, Wagnerian *L'Embrace*. Indeed, six of Brancusi's sculptures have the same title as six of Rodin's; we can advance a long way into understanding what modernism is all about by comparing these works. It was George Braque's understanding that cubism was correcting some excess or loss of direction in academic painting. Pound and Eliot responded to each other throughout their careers. *The Pisan Cantos* are a reply to the *Four Quartets*; Eliot's "Coriolan" is a reply to the Malatesta Cantos; *Prufrock* and *Mauberley* are voices in antiphony, and both poets do a "Portrait d'une Femme" as if they were Braque and Picasso working in the same studio.

These are conscious counterstatements. If Lévi-Strauss is right, all art is an answer, whether it knows it or not. The question may be one that confronts two artists simultaneously, as when in the same year Margaret Mitchell gave us *Gone with the Wind* and Faulkner, *Absalom Absalom*: diametrically opposed accounts of southern life. *Candide* and *Rasselas* share this same eerie simultaneity. Can we explain our neglect of Doughty's *The Dawn in Britain* by its being published the same year as Hardy's *The Dynasts*? Art is not excused from accidents. We chose Mozart over Salieri, we chose Shelley's "Ozymandias" over Horace Smith's sonnet "On a Stupendous Leg of Granite Standing All Alone in the Desert," to which Shelley was replying, and on the same page of a newspaper, Alain de Lilles and Bernardus Silvestris, *Prometheus Unbound* and *Frankenstein, or the Modern Prometheus* (a rare example of response between husband and wife); William Carlos Williams' *Paterson* is obviously a reply to Pound's *Cantos*, and Louis Zukofsky's *"A"* is a reply to both.

Art, as Harry Levin has said, and with much brilliance shown, is its own historian. It is also its own critic. It can sustain centuries of praise, as with *Don Quixote*, while we can accept all its imitators, from Fielding to Flaubert, as commentary on that great book. All emulation honors. We live in, or seem to live in, a century whose art summarizes, or explores to the limits of art, forms developed in other times. Opposing works of art, if only as original and parody, are as old as art itself, as witness Euripides and Aristophanes. Or Alain de Lille and Bernardus Silvestris, with their two poems taking opposite sides in the mediaeval debate as to whether God wants us to fulfill ourselves in the world, or use it as a stepping-stone to Heaven. Jules Laforgue's *Les fleurs de bonne volonté* answers Baudelaire's *Les fleurs du mal*. The imaginary space between these two masterpieces is criticism's stage—a space where the horizons east and west might be seen as philosophical melancholy debating with religious melancholy, or two aesthetic masks of the world, like those of comedy and tragedy in traditional iconography, set side by side.

The critic is perhaps first of all a spectator at a contest, where we are all natural critics, preferring this boxer's style over his challenger's, learning an abstract art of boxing (on which we can write a treatise) unknown to Boxer A or Boxer B. The first benefit of criticism is the overview, or privileged knowledge.

Melville's *Billy Budd* answers Hawthorne's *The Marble Faun*. Michel Tournier's *Friday* answers *Robinson Crusoe*. There is a discernible tradition of dialogue among works of narrative art, as indeed amongst all the arts. Charles Ives' Fourth Symphony answers Beethoven's Ninth; his *Robert Browning Overture* comments on qualities in Browning which literary criticism, in prose, cannot command. We must stand back a bit, for perspective's sake, to see the enormity of the strategy of response in the twentieth century. *The Odyssey* has elicited three masterful responses—Joyce's *Ulysses*, Pound's *Cantos*, Kazantzakis' *Odysseia*. Having observed this, we can look with suspicion at other writers. We have a modern *Iliad* in T. E. Lawrence's *Seven Pillars of Wisdom*, and we note that he translated the *Odyssey*. He was perhaps emulating with unconscious intent his hero Charles Montagu Doughty, who gave us an *Odyssey* in his *Travels in Arabia Deserta* and an *Iliad* in his great *Dawn in Britain*. Lesser writers exhibit Homeric plans:

William Saroyan in a whimsical novel about growing up in California, for a lesser example.

Translations of Homer run parallel to emulations and evocation of him—a classical counterbalance to native impulses to make epics in more eccentric ways. In this pattern we can see a geography: Homer is always a radiation from the Mediterranean. These radial lines, moving north, bounce back, changed by their encounter. So that beside Chapman's Homer we have *The Faerie Queene*, which has dipped twice in the Mediterranean, once for classical imagery and matter, once for the chivalric epic as written by Tasso and Boiardo (itself containing reverberations from the North). Pope's translation of Homer takes a French road to the Mediterranean; nineteenth-century translations do a double loop, echoing Biblical diction and flourishing Miltonic phrasings, both of which traditions are webs of connections between the North and the Mediterranean.

This attention to Homer is not only retrospective; it is a communal effort in literature to unify its vision. It wants to know what it is. Ancient accounts tell us that Lycurgus (if there was a Lycurgus), in setting out to make a work of art of the state, his native Sparta, found the Homeric poems on his travels to study government and pure morals. With some reservations about them, but recognizing them as the best poetry he could find, he introduced them into Sparta as the basis of education. Centuries later, Diogenes would remark that it is an impertinence for Athenian professors to lecture on Homer. For what Lycurgus saw in Homer was a nobility of spirit.

It is perhaps that nobility, so lost and almost unimaginable, that has made Homer our choice for the beginning of Western literature. He also supplies a symmetrical alternative to the Old Testament, which is just as rich in narrative, has the same kind of intercourse between man and god, but lacks the neutrality of Homer. Strangely, their literalness of geography and of personages has been established neck and neck by archeology and scholarship. An early Victorian intellectual could consider Abraham and Nestor equally fabulous. And then archeology embarrassed him by finding the city in which each lived. The past has an authenticity now that it has never enjoyed before.

A work of art easily offers us three angles of interest: how it came to be, what it is, and how the world has honored or neglected it. "To understand how the artist felt [in his act of creation]," as Santayana has said, "is not criticism; criticism is an investigation of what the work is good for." How a work came to be has fascinated critics, and all of us are reluctant to dismiss the study of origins from the concerns of criticism. Geoffrey Bullough's eight volumes of the *Narrative and Dramatic Sources of Shakespeare*—4,500 pages—cannot be wholly useless to the critic. In them we learn that after Laird and Lady Macbeth (whose name turns out to be Gruoch) had substracted their cousin Duncan from the line of succession to the throne, they went on a vacation (or possibly pilgrimage) to the Continent, as far as Rome. This diversion of the Macbeths has no interest for Shakespeare; but it catches our attention. We know another detail of Shakespeare's shaping of his matter into a rigorous unity.

Art is the great abbreviator of experience into vivid symbols. It is art that focuses George Washington's childhood into a moment with a hatchet, a cherry tree, and a patrician father. Parson Weems is the Plutarch who invented this moment, and it is futile for the careful historian to say that cherry trees had not yet been introduced into Virginia. Santayana, when he asked that criticism not claim to be doing something worthwhile in backtracking the way that led to creation, was thinking of the emotions, not the matter, involved in the making of a work of art. Artists themselves delight in mythologizing about moments of creation. We know how Shelley came to write "Ozymandias"—in a few minutes, to rival a friend's sonnet on the same subject—how Coleridge lost the rest of "Kubla Khan"—interrupted by "the man from Porlock"—how Tennyson scribbled "Crossing the Bar" on an envelope in his pocket, in a surge of inspiration.

There is another kind of study of origins that has nothing to do with romantic inspiration. The artist can be unconscious of forces which he imagines he is commanding but which are commanding him. Plutarch, writing his Life of Marcus Furius Camillus, the fourth-century B.C. Roman military genius who was considered the second founder of Rome after its defeat by the Gauls in 390, must have felt that he was far from the mythologized figures, such as Romulus and Theseus, of the early *Lives*, where even the most talented Greek credulity could scarcely discern the outlines of actual people, or even an historical moment that could be made to coincide with an epic time containing centaurs, Cretan monsters, and erotic encounters with gods. Camillus lived in a landscape of real cities. He fought and vanquished real people. A touch of the mythological may have crept in, by way of assimilated folktale, in the matter of the lake that rose in the mountains and threatened to flood Italy if, as the oracle said, Camillus did not do such and such. He did, and the overflow of the lake was contained in a river. Otherwise, we have historical narrative in Plutarch's account. But do we? The French scholar Georges Dumézil became suspicious of what Plutarch so carefully records: that all of Camillus' battles (like those of the First World War) began at dawn, to surprise a sleeping enemy. He then noticed that Camillus dedicated a temple to a goddess who has not survived in our consciousness of the Roman pantheon, Mater Matuta, goddess of the dawn. The more Dumézil studied Plutarch's biography of Camillus, the more the details of his life melted into myth. We can find part of the myth in Irish folklore, part in a lost Roman myth that can be reconstructed. Roman historians had already noticed a suspicious symmetry in Camillus' victories, accounting for this by the patrician Roman habit of touching up history for both dramatic and political reasons. After Dumézil's study, however, we are free to doubt that any such person as Camillus lived on this earth. A whole biography by Plutarch disappears. But then Dumézil has made practically all of Roman history disappear, so that we are left dumbfounded, facing a great blank that we had thought was the history of Rome.

The study of origins, then, can claim a strong place in criticism. History steadily gives way to literature. We are now aware that the heroic photographs in *Life* magazine of General MacArthur wading ashore at Leyte and Luzon were carefully staged afterwards, when the event, or non-event, could be photographed in safety and with a regard for composition. Eisenhower was reading a Louis L'Amour western while the troops landed on the Normandy beaches on D day, and Roosevelt was halfway through a Perry Mason detective novel when he died—trivial facts, we say, of the kind that sentimental journalism has taught us to savor. But we can identify them as details that may well lose their innocence in the hands of future historians. We cannot imagine what an historian a thousand years hence will make of them. Soviet history has been mythologized from its beginning, and is constantly under revision.

Literary genetics has its problems and surprises. There are many unsuspected instigations we would have been a long time discovering: it was Thomas Mann's reading of Conrad, together with Harry Levin's study of Joyce (Mann could not read Joyce himself) that led to the composition of *Doktor Faustus*, a book which we might have thought was the one work Mann was born to write, every line of it being implicit in his previous novels and stories. Because the writing of the Swiss novelist Robert Walser remained unknown and unstudied for so long, we have missed the origins of themes taken over and developed by Hermann Hesse (*The Glassbead Game*), Mann (*Felix Krull*), and Kafka (*Amerika, The Metamorphosis*), all of which come as ideas from Walser's *Jacob von Gunten*, a novel about being a servant, about monotony, about the enslavement of time by money. Walser was the Paul Klee of writing, when he was at his most imaginative, and a Christian Kafka who saw the human condition at its greyest average. His life was wholly disorganized, collapsing from temporary job to temporary job, until age thirty-five, when he enrolled in a school for butlers, having decided that subservience is our only true freedom. His next decision, after various stints as a butler, was to move into an insane asylum—the phrase "paranoid schizophrenia" was coined for his condition, and was immediately useful to describe that of another patient in the asylum, whose name was Nijinsky, who had been a dancer and was now, as he explained, a horse. Walser lived out the rest of his long life in the asylum, saying that all writers had failed, for what success could they claim as civilizing forces in the world of Hitler and Stalin?

This renunciation of writing by so gifted a genius is one of the tragedies of our time, to be put beside the loss of Walter Benjamin, Mandelstam, Khlebnikov, and Federico García Lorca. And yet we have just learned that Walser did not entirely quit. His friend Carl Seelig, who has left us an account of Walser's time in the asylum (recording his conversations on walks with him), discovered that Walser had written, in a tiny hand, on the backs of calendars and scrap paper elegant and fanciful little paragraphs, which have been published as the *Micrographia* of Robert Walser.

Tracking literary descent has its own problems. Consider this example: there are seven poems by Yeats concerned with an old woman whom he at first named Crazy Mary, later Crazy Jane, one of Yeats' most felicitous inventions. She is a Brechtian soul, foulmouthed, deep-dyed in sin and dirt. She has a Blakean mind, and when she delivers her greatest lines,

> A woman can be proud and stiff
> When on love intent;
> But Love has pitched his mansion in
> The place of excrement;
> For nothing can be sole or whole
> That has not been rent,

she is paraphrasing a line of *Jerusalem*. This is from "Crazy Jane Talks with the Bishop," in *The Winding Stair* of 1933, and is a companion poem to "Crazy Jane and the Bishop" where it is deliciously uncertain whether "the solid man and the coxcomb" refers to Jane's disreputable lover Jack and the bishop, or the other way round. In his own eyes, the bishop is the solid man, Jack the coxcomb. Jane thinks otherwise.

We have in these sprightly, savagely ironic poems a sharp propaganda for the instincts over their restraint by gentility, and Yeats himself has given us many notes on the origins of the poems, citing a real old woman known to him and Lady Gregory. We can recognize in Jane an Irish type dear to Synge and even Joyce (imagine Molly Bloom old). The meter of all the Crazy Jane poems is a kind of Irish jig, and one of them is devoted to dancers who leap.

In 1889, the year of Yeats' first book, *Crossways* (remember that title), George Meredith wrote a poem called "Jump-to-Glory-Jane" and published it in *The Universal Review*. Meredith was thinking of a Mrs. Mary Ann Girling, a religious fanatic about whom Laurence Housman wrote his novel *The Sheepfold* (1918). Meredith was also thinking about Shakers and Methodists in the United States, who expressed religious joy in shouting and dancing. The poem begins:

> A revelation came on Jane,
> The widow of a labouring swain:
> And first her body trembled sharp,
> Then all the woman was a harp
> With wind along the strings; she heard
> Though there was neither tone nor word.

For thirty-six jouncing stanzas Jane jumps, joined by other jumpers, silently, untiringly. The jumping was to purify to the point of ecstasy, and to admonish the smug and sedate.

> And she within herself had sight
> Of Heaven at work to cleanse outright,
> To make of her a mansion fit
> For angel hosts inside to sit.
>
> They entered, and forthwith entranced,
> Her body braced, her members danced;
> Surprisingly the woman leapt;
> And countenance composed she kept . . .
>
> A good knee's height, they say, she sprang;
> Her arms and feet like those who hang:
> As if afire the body sped,
> And neither pair contributed.
> She jumped in silence: she was thought
> A corpse to resurrection brought.

Jane's dancing is contagious. She soon has a troop of jumpers with her, mainly the old who had not thought they could spring, and higher and higher.

> When turnips were a filling crop,
> In scorn they jumped a butcher's shop:
> Or, spite of threats to flog and souse,
> They jumped for shame a public house:
> And much their legs were seized with rage
> If passing by the vicarage.

The vicarage. It is the established church that becomes the focus of Jane's campaign of jumping. When the Squire has a harvest feast in a tent, the Bishop comes to bless it, and Jane comes "to show the way to grace."

> In apron suit the Bishop stood;
> The crowding people kindly viewed.
> A gaunt grey woman he saw rise
> On air, with most beseeching eyes . . .

> Her highest leap had come: with ease
> She jumped to reach the Bishop's knees:
> Compressing tight her arms and lips,
> She sought to jump the Bishop's hips:
> Her aim flew at his apron-band,
> That he might see and understand.

Jane mimes a sermon for the worldly Bishop:

> In jumps that said, Beware the pit!
> More eloquent than speaking it—
> That said, Avoid the boiled, the roast;
> The heated nose on face of ghost,
> Which comes of drinking, up and o'er
> The flesh with me! did Jane implore.

Her message is Quakerish: she wants him to doff his Bishop's suit and dance as naked and innocent as a babe. But

> He gave no sign of making bare,
> Nor she of faintness or despair.

The Bishop is about to catch the contagion, and to jump, when the outraged Squire drives Jane and her dancers from his land. As for the Bishop,

> he was lost: a banished face
> For ever from the ways of grace.

Meredith (like Yeats) is wholly on Jane's side, and moralizes when she dies in a mighty leap:

> May those who ply the tongue that cheats,
> And those who rush to beer and meats,
> And those whose mean ambition aims
> At palaces and titled names,
> Depart in such a cheerful strain
> As did our Jump-to-Glory Jane!
>
> Her end was beautiful: one sigh.
> She jumped a foot when it was nigh.
> A lily in a linen clout
> She looked when they had laid her out.
> It is a lily-light she bears
> For England up the ladder-stairs.

Years later, when Yeats was creating Crazy Jane, surely he was remembering Meredith's poem. It is a poem equivalent to the eccentric religious painting of Stanley Spencer, who painted the Bible as if it all happened in the village of Cookham-on-Thames. It is a poem in a long tradition in English culture, where religion seems to thrive best in homemade forms, like those of Blake and Christopher Smart, John Bunyan and John Milton.

The people who keep track of such things have not connected Meredith's Jane with Yeats' Jane because they need another kind of evidence. They also need a wider view of poetry. (I could simply say that Meredith scholars don't read Yeats and Yeats scholars don't read Meredith because of territorial imperatives, but I won't.)

What's happening here is a process I like to call finishing, not in the sense of culminating, but of polishing. Art as a continuity is given to refining, to remaking with greater economy and sharper effect. Yeats was remembering, half consciously let us say, Meredith's poem. It is Victorian, long-winded; it has the old energy of when people had more time to read. Yeats modernized it, while making it wholly his own. Meredith was locating comedy in seriousness; Yeats, seriousness in comedy. Both poets are wearing masks. Yeats, it has been said, would believe anything sufficiently incredible; speaking through Crazy Jane, he can believe the incredible in comfort, and offer it with salt.

The genetic components of a work of art are responses, both of agreement and of modification. Spontaneous generation is as uncommon in art as in nature. When, in 1904, O. Henry published his first book, and only novel, he was already the skilled writer of short stories we know him to be. It was the young Witter Bynner who showed O. Henry how to link a suite of stories into a consecutive plot, an invention useful later to Sherwood Anderson in *Winesburg, Ohio*, and to Eudora Welty in *The Golden Apples*. The sections of O. Henry's *Cabbages and Kings* are not strictly short stories, and they are not strictly chapters in a novel. They comply whimsically to motifs specified in "The Walrus and the Carpenter":

> "The time has come," the Walrus said,
> "To talk of many things:
> "Of shoes—and ships—and sealing wax—
> "Of cabbages—and kings—

It takes a tall tale, gratuitously introduced in the pure spirit of comedy to get shoes into the plot (Faulkner and Mark Twain were addicted to such high jinks, for the sheer fun of the joke). O. Henry's Anchurians—that is, Hondurans—did not wear shoes, but a slick shoe salesman from Alabama imported tons of cockleburs and on a dark night spread them over the grassy streets of Coralia. There are ships aplenty, for the entrances and exits of all the characters. There are potentates who will serve for kings. Once an author has chosen a family of references, he is obliged to account for them, as Spenser was to account for a set of virtues in *The Faerie Queene*, or Joyce, in *Ulysses*, for all the adventures of Odysseus, the organs of the body, the letters of the Irish alphabet, the stations of the cross, and so on. O. Henry omits cabbages, and in looking for them we begin to smile, for whereas he tips us off as to who the Carpenter is, namely himself, the architect of the devilishly complex plot, he is silent about the Walrus. The Walrus, quite plausibly, is the American Secretary of War at the time, William Howard Taft, whose physique and moustache were eminently suggestive of walruses, and who was the shaper of the gunboat diplomacy that kept Honduran affairs compliant to the will of the United Fruit Company. The cabbages, then, are (in the immemorial symbolism of New Comedy) the Anchurians themselves.

Charles Lutwidge Dodgson, whose name in the looking-glass gives Lutwidge Charles, which, run through Latin, French, and Norman English—that is, an historically reverse etymology—gives us Lewis Carroll, was, as O. Henry chose also, a man with a name to hide behind in an open secret. O. Henry was hiding in earnest, but, as with all his plot manoeuvres, the truth is there to see, or there for the clever to see. O. Henry is a set of letters which can be discovered in consecutive order in *Ohio* State Penite*ntiary*. Knowing this, we can look back at *Cabbages and Kings* and appreciate how close to the bone its plot is. A Honduran president absconds with the treasury, for the love of a woman. Another character, with whom the president is consistently confused (through a legerdemain of a narrative trick) and who is president of the Republic Insurance Company (allowing O. Henry to achieve perfect New Comedy confusion in the phrase "President of the Republic"), has made off with the exact large amount of money, carried in the same style of valise, as the President of the Republic of Anchuria. Now O. Henry was in Honduras fleeing the authorities in Austin, Texas, who wanted him for embezzlement. Even now, we are not certain if the charge was just, but O. Henry served his time, and wrote *Cabbages and Kings*, where the spirit of the work is mistaken guilt.

What is of greater interest to the critic, however, is that this novel was written in 1904—a year that had seen earlier the publication of Conrad's *Nostromo*, a novel set in as imaginary a South American republic as O. Henry's—and is about the disappearance and recovery of an enormous sum of money, is about revolutions and loyalties and love. O. Henry, it would seem, was in addition to all his other reasons, rewriting *Nostromo*. He was, indeed, translating it. To put the two novels before us is to have a lesson in literary genetics. Conrad's novel is masterful and inventive. It is a study in the psychology of integrity, in the psychology of the passions. And its narrative method is to conceal the relationship among events until they are disclosed in a resolution of surprise.

Criticism is reluctant to place O. Henry and Conrad together, for good reasons and for bad. Conrad is in a tradition; he has behind him, we feel, the immense authority of his Slavic origins. He is legitimately kin, in whatever way, to Dostoievski and Turgenev. He stands shoulder to shoulder with Henry James and Flaubert. His credentials are respectful. O. Henry, on the other hand, is of suspect origin. His first service to the American language was to give a name to Vicks Salve, which was invented in Greensboro, N.C. Not to mention a candy bar named for him.

When *Nostromo* and *Cabbages and Kings* were published in 1904, we were beginning to make a distinction not among the four large types of literature which Northrop Frye has named comedy, romance, tragedy, and satire, or spring, summer, autumn, and winter spirits of the imagination, but between comic and serious. Some writers, like Shakespeare, Mark Twain, and Bernard Shaw, were allowed to be both at once, but with the understanding that the comic was being put in the service of the serious. The seriousness of the comic writer could only be sentimentality, and his business was to entertain, not to instruct.

Dickens died a decade before the establishment of English departments in universities, so that he did not have to suffer professorial debates about serious and comic literature, though he had quite enough of it from the critics. And literature itself was making the distinction. There is much comedy in Conrad, but we have to rephrase that for dichotomy's sake, and say that with all his seriousness he had a sense of humor (one of the British virtues, we must understand), so that a comic work like *Typhoon* still gets classified as serious.

We do not normally see Conrad as one of Dickens' offspring, even when we have to admit that Dostoievski and Proust were; but he was.

Chance, published in 1913, was Conrad's first popular success. His critical reputation had long been established; indeed, his masterpieces—*The Nigger of the Narcissus* (1897), *Lord Jim* (1900), *Nostromo* (1904), *The Secret Agent* (1907), together with the best of the stories and short novels—had been written. Most critics see in *Chance* a decline, the beginning of the later manner which was reminiscent of his early powers, rather than a repetition of them. But the public liked it: there was something in this new novel that was familiar and congenial. The exotic is removed. The characters are British and contemporary. The plot is still thoroughly Conradian: in shifting planes of narrative that overlap just enough for us, chapter by chapter, to see not the unfolding of a plot, but new revelations in a plot that has been before our eyes all along—it's just that, as with Henry James' and Conrad's great emulator, Ford Madox Ford, we don't understand what we are seeing.

Lifted away from the subtleties of Conrad's narration, out of its frame of a story within a story within a story, the plot is something like this. A London financier, one de Barral, has built a fraudulent empire of savings banks. The empire falls, and he goes to prison for bilking the public of millions. His daughter Flora is left to lower-class relatives to be looked after. Miserable, she strikes out to make her fortune in various humble ways, as a governess, as a lady's companion, all failures, and comes under the wing of a pair of ineffectual liberals and women's liberationists who proceed to wreck her life even more thoroughly than had the slings and arrows of fortune itself.

She is saved by a noble-hearted sea captain, whose wife she becomes. (Here I must omit a psychological dimension of the novel, and this omission is pretty much like omitting the strings and horns from a Beethoven symphony.) The captain and Flora generously give a home—on board the captain's ship—to Flora's father when his prison term is over. But old de Barral resents his son-in-law, feeling that his daughter has betrayed him by marrying while he was behind bars. Furthermore, he considers his home aboard ship as another prison. He attempts to murder the captain with poison he had meant to take at the time of his conviction. In one of Conrad's hair-raising denouements, de Barral succeeds only in killing himself. The ambiguities of Flora and the captain's marriage are resolved: she had been led to believe by a deceptive letter that the captain pitied rather than loved her, and the captain had believed that Flora did not love him but had married him for protection, and to have a home for her ruined father. The story goes on, with some lovely extra turns of the screw.

The novel is perhaps Conrad's final word on the duplicities of life on land and the clarities and loyalties of life on the sea. It is also his definitive marker drawn between sails and steam, the old order of honor and the new order of money.

If Conrad's critics missed the contrast between civilization and the primitive, and the heroism of man against the elements, what the public was reacting to was the fact, which no one has noticed, that Conrad was rewriting a novel by Dickens. *Chance* is a translation, into another style, of *Dombey and Son*, just as O. Henry's *Cabbages and Kings* was a translation into New Comedy of the romantically tragic *Nostromo*.

The title *Chance* begins the critical interplay: Dickens articulates his plot with coincidences. The problem of coincidences is that they must be plausible, must, in whatever sense, be possible in the given circumstances of time and locale. They must, most of all, be called into being by character, which, for Dickens as for Heraclitus, is fate. Dombey's meanness must be the prime mover of his downfall. Around him we have generosities, romantic love, hypocrisies, betrayals, good natures, good intentions brutalized by poverty and vice. All of these arrange the network of coincidences which we call the plot. But, Conrad seems to have asked himself if life is not a matter of *inci*-dences, of random events and pressures, rather than of coincidences. In this idea we can see the instigation to rewrite a Dickens novel with the accidental given the value of a character, in which the implausible is shown with the power it really has.

The plot of *Dombey* is a crossing of long roads; the plot of *Chance* is a backtracking to where unseen crossroads were concealed from us when we passed them. Conrad's study of Flaubert was visual and psychological; we must add to it his equally careful study of Guy de Maupassant, which may, on closer inspection, be a study of Dickens, whom he read early, and in Polish.

For Captain Cuttle's role as factotum, Conrad has Marlowe, who is not so much the ideal narrator as Conrad's ideal reader—a spectator inside the story. He is, like Captain Cuttle, our representative on scene. This is the only character whom Conrad leaves in place. With a magnificent economy, Conrad compresses Dickens' picturesque dockside characters into two Dickensian grotesques in ill-fitting clothes. De Barral is made to contain both Dombey and Carker, a monster of finance, a man who is all self. Flora is simply Florence reseen, and with all the advantages of Dickensian awe of the female, and of sentimentality, subtracted. We can guess that Conrad must have whispered to himself that he wanted to supply flesh and blood for Dickensian cardboard.

There is a tip of the hand at the end of chapter 6 of *Chance*. Marlowe is talking. "I remembered what Mrs. Fyne had told me before of the view she had years ago of de Barral clinging to the child [his daughter Flora] at the side of his wife's grave and later on of these two walking hand in hand the observed of all eyes by the sea. Figures from Dickens—pregnant with pathos."

By the sea. Dickens had made his distinction between land characters, all bad, and sea characters, all good. Florence is the one character who is transferred from land to sea; she marries a sailor; she puts off the taint of the land. Her child is born at sea. This demarcation may be what interested Conrad in the first place, for he shared Dickens' irrational intuition about sea and land, and compounded it with another demarcation between sailing ships and steam.

Steam in Dickens is the railroad, a vengeful implement, just as a steamship is the final embodiment of fate in *Chance*. Dickens' acknowledgment of the irrational is in the totemistic shop sign The Wooden Midshipman, who operates something like Queequeg's little black idol, whose kind Dickens had in mind when he wrote "But no fierce idol with a mouth from ear to ear, and a murderous visage made of parrot's feathers, was ever more indifferent to the appeals of its savage votaries. . . ." And: "[The Wooden Midshipman] was so far a creature of circumstances, that a dry day covered him with dust, and a misty day peppered him with little bits of soot, and a wet day brightened up his tarnished uniform for a moment, and a very hot day blistered him; but otherwise he was a callous, obdurate, conceited midshipman, intent on his own discoveries, and caring as little for what went on about him, terrestrially, as Archimedes at the taking of Syracuse."

Unable to express the futility of religion in a popular romance, Dickens symbolizes it in a thoroughly archaic totem, which nevertheless works with a full measure of superstition—the nautical implements made by Solomon Gills (note the fishiness of the name) turn out to be ahead of their time, and the cause of wealth. Conrad's tangent upon the unknown is more abstract:

"The surprise," Marlowe says, "it is easy to understand, would arise from the inability to interpret aright the signs which experience (a thing mysterious in itself) makes to our understanding and emotions. For it is never more than that. Our experience never gets into our blood and bones. It always remains outside of us. That's why we look with wonder at the past."

Dickens has no true ancestors. He takes narrative technique from Smollett and Fielding, he takes tone from Surtees and Cervantes. He is gloriously self-invented. He wrote with the passion of a primitive storyteller, trusting to genius to show him how his troupe of actors would interact. Ultimately, however, he looked to blind faith in something—human nature, a primitive idol—to lead him and his readers through experience which "always remains outside of us."

The arts are a way of internalizing experience, allowing us to look with wonder at a past that is not ours, but enough of ours so that all stories are, as Joyce says, always "the same anew." It is not therefore surprising that the best books are old books rewritten. The tribe has its tales.

So there we are. Where else could we be?

The Scholar as Critic

Let us begin with difficulties. Between 1911 and 1914 James Joyce wrote paragraphs and sentences in a notebook, one of several in which he tried out prose styles, descriptions, bits of dialogue. This notebook is the exact equivalent of a painter's sketchpad. What it contains is best described by the word *jottings*. Joyce was eminently a jotter. *Ulysses*, the composition of which was underway in these years, was precipitated from many such notebooks, and we have the early worksheets of *Finnegans Wake*, many of which are simply lists of words: preparations of the palette, and of underdrawing, before the real work.

Because this notebook had an oblong label with a nice red border, rounded at the edges, on its front cover, where one might write *conti* or *ricetti*, or one's name, Joyce wrote *Giacomo Joyce*, a wholly rational and useful thing to do.

When Joyce left Trieste, he threw this notebook away, or at least left it behind. His brother Stanislaus latched onto it as something to save. In 1968 the Joyce scholar and biographer Richard Ellmann, Goldsmith Professor of English at the University of Oxford, published the notebook as a work of fiction by Joyce, and claimed that it is a long-lost masterpiece. The event made the front page of the *New York Times*. A limited edition was offered the discriminating public. Most scholars knew about this notebook (Ellmann quotes from it in his biography, and it is the source of our knowledge of a sentimental wandering of Joyce's eye, about which the less said the better).

There is no work of fiction by James Joyce named *Giacomo Joyce*, though the Oxford University Press keeps it in print, and as late as last week was still advertising it as Joyce's long-lost masterpiece, the one found by Professor Ellmann. What, we may well ask, is going on here? Well, it is a great thing to find a lost work. The world's last copy of Catullus was found in the Renaissance, used by monks to bung a wine-barrel. Most of an ancient copy of the book of Isaiah was found by a shepherd chunking rocks into a cave in Israel, by way of boredom. Boswell's diaries turned up in our day in a trunk in an attic. A cagey Victorian once bought Aristotle's constitution for the city of Athens from an Arab in the back streets of Cairo, who said he found it somewhere. The history of discoveries is the scholar's portion of high adventure.

Professor Ellmann had missed one opportunity to find a lost manuscript of Joyce's. He himself recorded in his biography all the details a literary detective would need to track down a set of examination papers Joyce wrote in April 1912, when he was trying to land a position at the University of Padua (he didn't get it). What Prof. Ellmann didn't guess was that they never throw anything away in Italy. So that when Louis Berrone, of Fairfield University, hied himself to Padua, on a wild hunch, and asked the archivist at the University of Padua if he could see a set of examination papers written back in 1912 by a job candidate name of Joyce, the archivist replied, "Certamente," and went and got them.

These exam papers are published. But as what they are, not as a long lost novel by the century's greatest writer. I am not aware of any strenuous objection to Ellmann's fancied lost work, and I worry about innocent students coming across it, as yet ignorant of *Dubliners*, the *Portrait*, *Ulysses* and *Finnegans Wake*, and being misled by a scholar of great repute into thinking that they are reading Joyce.

Let us stick with Joyce and his scholars and critics for a while. Just recently the German scholar Hans Gabler published a definitive edition of *Ulysses*. The text of this masterpiece, we have always known, has never been set correctly. Its original printers were French, the firm of Darantière in Dijon. Edition after edition made feeble attempts to correct the thousands of typographical errors that had crept in, and to restore sentences that had been lost or garbled in the many states of the text as it went from typists to the little magazines where much of the text was first published.

The most ambitious—and successful—attempt to establish a text of *Ulysses* was made in 1975 by Clive Driver, for the Rosenbach Foundation, which owns a fair copy which Joyce (and, in places, the whole Joyce family), made to sell to the Rosenbachs. Here we have a facsimile of the manuscript, together with the text marked with proofreader's corrections (these are Driver's), so that we can see at a glance all revisions and restorations.

At line 6 of chapter 15 ("Circe") the phrase "lumps of coal and copper snow" occurs—a description of cones of ice with fruit-juice flavoring, where coal and copper are color adjectives, presumably for grape and orange flavors.

In 1929 a French translation of *Ulysses* was published by Auguste Morel, "assisté par M. Stuart Gilbert" (Joyce's first explicator, and a close friend). Moreover this translation was, as the title page says, "entièrement revue par M. Valéry Larbaud avec la collaboration de l'auteur." That's a committee of four, two sensitive and accomplished translators, and two watchdogs of keenest attention, one of them being Joyce himself. In 1929 *Ulysses* was still banned in all English-speaking countries, but here was a text for the French, who only ban political books. In this text the phrase we are looking at, "lumps of coal and copper snow" comes out as "des couches d'une neige de charbon et de cuivre"—not *neige de corail*. *Charbon*, coal. Despite this evidence to the contrary, Driver in the Rosenbach recension decided from Joyce's scrawled handwriting that Joyce had written *coral*, not *coal*.

Gabler follows Driver, and emends *coal* to *coral* in his definitive text. This little contention over a single word in a very big text gives us a chance to ask what a scholar is doing when he emends a text. Driver is pleading the authority of his eyes (I, for one, am not convinced: Joyce has written *coal*, it seems to me). And here is where we must say that a textual critic must know the meaning of the words he is emending.

The "Circe" chapter of *Ulysses* is a descent into the underworld. Bloom is Orpheus; his being, as continued in his son Rudy (who died as a child), is his Eurydice. He cannot reclaim him, but he begins a new idea of fatherhood by befriending Stephen. The symbolism is extraordinarily rich: the chapter is a Temptation of St. Anthony, a harrowing of Hell by Christ, a *Walpurgisnacht*, a dark night of the soul. But all the symbolism is of things underground, not of things undersea. There is sea symbolism in many places in *Ulysses*, in the first, third, sixteenth, and eighteenth chapters, but not here. Coral, we should be in a scholarly position to say, is of the wrong family of symbols; coal of the right family. We can cite a parallel case. The first emendation most of us learned about as undergraduates is the one in the description by Mistress Quickly of Falstaff's death:

> after I saw him fumble with the Sheets, and play with Flowers, and smile upon his fingers end, I knew there was but one way: for his Nose was as sharp as a Pen, and a Table of greene fields.

Take "for his Nose was as sharp as a Pen" as a parenthetical remark, such as the language of grief, trying to describe a moment of deep emotion, might interpolate, and the sentence can be understood as "I saw him fumble with the Sheets, and smile upon his fingers end and a Table of greene fields." That is, Falstaff had said, "I see Flowers and a Table of greene fields." These are his last words. By table he meant picture; Shakespeare uses it as the equivalent of *tableau* in two other places. The old rascal was convinced that he was going to heaven, as doubtless he was, and as he died he reported that he saw flowers and green fields as beautiful as a picture in a book.

But Shakespearean scholars rejoice that one of them emended this famous crux, as they think it, to "a babbled of greene fields." And for no other reason than that their ear could not follow the rhythm of grief.

Modern texts ought not, we think, be far more corrupt than ancient ones, but they are. Our texts for the *Iliad* and *Odyssey* are far better than those of Shakespeare. And as we improve in technology, we lose in human care. Not that technology doesn't have its own shortcomings. Just last week a novelist I know, and who likes to be up-to-date, called up the text he was working on, to get a blank screen on his word-processor. He then had to realize that he had lost seventy-five pages of a novel. Not even Professor Ellmann can ever find those seventy-five pages. They are so many random electrons floating around in Detroit.

The French have established a text for Proust, who never read proofs. Instead, he filled all that nice white space on the galleys with more text. Joyce's texts are where they are—and God will send us a hero to deal with *Finnegans Wake*. The greatest American modern master, Ezra Pound, will be the next undertaking of scholars who establish texts. The famous *Guide to Kulchur* (that is not Pound's title, but a frivolous one to annoy T. S. Eliot, who would have nothing to do with the original title), has an index that keeps referring to things that aren't any longer in the text, as page after page of libellous material was taken out in proof. Someday we will have the text as he wrote it. Someday someone will set *Hugh Selwyn Mauberley* correctly. Someday a scholar will reassemble a book by Pound called *I Gather the Limbs of Osiris*, which Pound himself broke up into essays and perhaps never finished. Someday we will be able to read a book of Pound's which our army destroyed all copies of, as it was being published together with Pound's translation into Italian of the *Ta Hio* of Confucius, "The Unwobbling Pivot." *Pivot* in Italian is *assis*, or axis, and some military scholar thought it was Fascist propaganda.

Someday we will have a text of *The Cantos*. At the moment three different versions are for sale. One is the Faber text available in England, another is the New Directions text, and the third is an *en face* text to Mary de Rachewiltz's Italian translation. The Italian text, for instance, prints the real names for which the Faber and New Directions texts still have pseudonyms. There are other differences, many of them as serious as the difference between the quarto and folio texts of Shakespeare. And there are interesting cruxes, such as Pound's mistakes. How, we ask, can a poem have mistakes? Well, Keats has Cortez discovering the Pacific, when he should have had Balboa, in the great sonnet on reading Chapman's Homer, and Chaucer has Alcibiades in a list of beautiful women. Joyce has Stephen Dedalus quoting from a book that wasn't published in 1904. As these anomalies recede in time, they gain quaintness. We forgive Euripides for telling us that the Egyptians lived in pyramids, and Sir Walter Scott for putting on a hilltop a French castle that's actually in a valley, and Victor Hugo for having Cromwell attending divine services in the Inner Temple of the Inns of Court.

But when Pound in *The Pisan Cantos* transliterates the Greek for night, νύξ as *nux*, and does not notice that this is the Latin for *nut*, we have the same kind of pedantic static as when a weary French translator saw ἄνευ as *aveu* (one of the eery few times a Greek word can be read as French). This blooper has been corrected, at least in the *en face* text to Eva Hesse's German translation. But what do we do with this?

In the *Pisan Cantos* we have this line:

> Pumpelly, "no dog, no goat"

This is Pound's ultimate style—as allusive as Chinese or Japanese for a court audience. These words are, in fact, intended to be radical elements in a complex ideogram. One pervasive image controls hundreds of lines. To read them, we need to understand the image, and then to calculate how each element is suspended in a field of force, like iron filings defining a magnetic field on a piece of paper. The context here is the perilous return of Odysseus to Ithaca on his raft. So Pound builds the ideogram of Odyssean details, or image rhymes, such as the poem has used all along. Raphael Pumpelly, the New Hampshire mining engineer, geologist, and archaeologist, went around the world pretty much by himself, in the early years of the century—his camel train passed that of Brooks Adams, Henry's brother, in the Gobi desert, and they did not speak, having never been introduced, and Pumpelly knowing what Bostonians are—and it is this circumambulation of the globe Pound thinks he is using as an Odyssean rhyme. Yet the phrase "no dog, no goat" refers to Captain Joshua Slocum, who sailed around the world in a sloop, without even a dog or a goat, as a dockhand in Gibraltar remarked when he put in there.

Pound's memory was like that, we can say, smugly. He makes the same kind of crisscrosses elsewhere—a polymath's honest mistakes. Achilles Fang's thesis on Pound catches him at hundreds of them. Would it not, however, be arrogant of an editor to emend the line to:

> Joshua Slocum, "no dog, no goat"

It cannot be done. Dante tried to fix the *Commedia* as firmly as he could, with a tight system of coordinates (number of lines, the terza rima itself, and layered and interlocking symbols)—a machine not to be tinkered with. You cannot easily insert a line to satisfy a whim, like the rich bibliophile who had an edition of *Paradise Lost* printed with an additional line saying that Adam and Eve brushed their teeth.

The scholar, then, is the transmitter of texts. He functions as a critic of the highest order because of his attention: what he chooses to edit, restore, annotate, reclaim. The tragic fragments that we have of archaic Greek poetry come to us from the archeologist, who knew where to dig, the classical scholar who then has to identify and transcribe—two of Sappho's editors went blind from trying to read blackened scraps of parchment and papyrus. A trove such as the Oxyrhynchus dig has rendered up a trash heap of papyrus fragments. Some are bills of lading, detailing a shipment of furniture and bath oil, some are pages of the Gospels. One is a letter from a little boy to his father, hinting that his behavior will be improved by interesting presents on an upcoming birthday.

Scholarly attention is an index of culture. We know what happened when Sir Herbert Grierson offered an edition of the English metaphysical poets, or when certain scholars at Tübingen gave us texts of the troubadours. Scholarship begins in somebody's imagination. Behind all the classical scholarship of the nineteenth century is an ideal kept bright by architects, poets, painters, collectors, amateurs, enthusiasts. The Classical spoke to some imaginative exultation in Winckelmann and Hölderlin, Shelley and the Brothers Adam. "Those who know nothing, love nothing; those who do nothing, understand nothing." Scholarship begins as a critical act of loving eyes: curiosity is passion. We can even assign nastily human ulterior motives, as passionate as noble ones, to the beginnings of scholarship. Housman's masterful edition of Manilius was an act of revenge, as well as a restoration of honor, to get back at Oxford, where Housman's tutor had simply forgotten to tell him that philosophy would be on his final exams. Pound's edition, with commentary, of Guido Cavalcanti, was done in hope that he could, after twenty-five years of procrastination, get his doctorate from Pennsylvania. Who knows what psychology is behind Mario Praz's monumental study of interiors, which take on a poignant meaning when we know that the belief that he had the Evil Eye made him a recluse.

In scholarship, criticism, and art we have an interchange of some complexity, and we would like to be able to see what it is, and how it works. There is the kind of student, or reader, who is thrown into indignation that pedantry should intervene between him and art, and goes so far as to accuse the critic and professor of living parasitically off art and literature. Wordsworth wrote, we read; we feel what Wordsworth felt. There are inquisitive students, however, who will ask when did this man live? What is Tintern Abbey? What is the reflex of a star?

Can we construct a model of cooperation among scholar, critic, and artist? Look at this. When Michael Faraday was working on electrolysis, he needed, as all scientists need, words. What Faraday did was walk across campus to consult the Master of Trinity College, Cambridge, the vastly accomplished Dr. William Whewell. And Whewell would say, "You ought to make these words out of Greek." Between them they came up with *ion*, *electrode*, *anode*, *cathode*. The ghost of Heraclitus attended these sessions. He had said you can go either way on a road, up it or down it, *ana* the *hodos* or *kata* the *hodos*, contracting into *anodos* and *kathodos*. One would like to hear these conversations, the continuation of Adam's naming the animals.

The definition in Johnson's dictionary of *electricity* is very elegant, nothing like his definition of *scorpion* ("a reptile much resembling a small lobster, but that his tail ends in a point with a very venomous sting"). A scholar of the history of science has recently ascertained that Johnson and Benjamin Franklin were both at a session of the Royal Society. It is plausible that, for all his distaste of Americans and revolutionaries, Johnson may well have approached Franklin with the offhanded gentleman's question, "Mr. Franklin, just what, in so many words, is electricity?"

So scholars communicate with scholars, sometimes coming to blows and unseemly shouting matches. They are not angels, and their humanity shows more than in ordinary mortals. We are told that R. Buckminster Fuller at George Gamow's table began to ask prying questions about solar physics. Gamow, European that he was, replied that they were eating: you don't talk shop while eating. Whereupon Fuller, transcendental philosopher, said that he was wasting his time at Gamow's table, and left. And there is a tale that a Turkish astronomer, wearing a fez, read a paper about a new asteroid at a scientific congress in Paris. No one paid any attention; the paper was not even recorded in the minutes. Next year, the Turkish astronomer read the same paper to the same congress, but without his fez, and was applauded warmly, and given a prize.

Critics and scholars are frequently the same person, or have offices side by side in universities. Their relationship to the artist can be comic, tragic, romantic, satiric. The howl of pain from classical scholars when Pound published his "Homage to Sextus Propertius" can still be heard. I have asked an Italian scholar for his opinion of Pound's edition of Cavalcanti. He replied with a single word, "Pitiful." Scholars as a phalanx of opinion are known to be resistant to change, and therefore inimical to the forward progress of their subject matter. The awesome struggle of modern painting and writing is still not appreciated. The Shakespeare scholar who also reads Joyce is rare. We are daily bedeviled by the breed of critic who feels that his perfected taste and an appeal to sweet reason qualify him to sit in judgment on anything. Mr. Schwarz of *The New Yorker* has recently called Caravaggio "tacky." Joyce's *Ulysses* was dismissed in 1922 by H. G. Wells, Bernard Shaw, Virginia Woolf, and Rebecca West. Sir Edmund Gosse wrote all important newspapers and journals, begging them to ignore it. Perhaps it would go away. We can compile an impressive list of artists who starved to death, like Velimir Khlebnikov, or committed suicide in despair, like van Gogh, because of rejection.

We are victimized weekly by bad criticism, and, by implication (as all criticism is informed by scholars), bad scholarship. It is my opinion that *The New York Review of Books*, that bastion of gratuitous meanness, has done more to discourage good writing in the United States than the Litkontrol branch of the Politburo has in the Soviet Union. And then there is the pernicious habit of the *New York Times Book Review* and the *Times Literary Supplement* of choosing reviewers with a vested interest in what they are reviewing. This makes for lively journalism, but for nothing else. For one thing, truly original writers must be omitted by this strategy, so that Ken Gangemi, Paul Metcalf, Jonathan Williams, August Kleinzahler, Nicholas Kilmer, Lorine Niedecker, Ronald Johnson, and the Lord he knoweth how many more, are not reviewed at all, and about them the scholars tend to be silent. We forget that William Carlos Williams got all the way to death's door before he was recognized as the great poet he was, and that Louis Zukofsky, whose name may well be the best known of our time when the dust has settled around the year 2050, remains unknown and unread.

The critic, then, is either not recognizing his power, or is failing us dreadfully. And behind his failure is that of the scholar.

From the scholar the artist asks this: that he constantly search the past, which is always fluid and in motion, because our attention is modified by the new and the old acting together. The recent success of Umberto Eco's *The Name of the Rose* made Europeans realize the goodness of narrative, and suddenly Victor Hugo and Jules Verne were respected writers again. Television and film, with their insatiable need for plots, have done more than the academy to revive an interest in the Victorians, for example. How many students have read Homer because of Joyce?

The principal concern binding the scholar, the critic, and the artist is the vital one of continuity. Culture is a continuum, because consciousness is a continuum. The only sensible definition of sanity is continuity of mind, no matter what the content. Physics is at the moment debating whether the universe is in discrete parts, like grains of sand contingent in a desert, or whether it is a continuous mass of neutrinos in which atomic particles are gross clots. It has been the genius of our century to begin to connect what had seemed to be abrupt discontinuities of culture into whole fabrics, the vertical dimension being history and time; the horizontal being geographical and diffusionist. Anthropology gave up its study of long influence about fifty years ago, as it was driving everyone mad and seducing orderly minds into silly theories. As an outsider, I am free to look back with at least an amused curiosity at this retreat of scholarship. I agree with the linguists when they put their foot down and forbade any paper on the origin of language at conferences. They were turning away squadrons of benign lunatics. The largest kind of mail received by scientific journals is from kitchen scientists who can prove Einstein and Darwin to have been mistaken. Banned as they are from academic discourse, the diffusionists did not desist. Their problem is not that they are wrongheaded, but that they cannot reach the high standards science must maintain. (To make my point, let us remember the amateur archeologist who unearthed a pottery shard in Tennessee, spent years trying to identify the inscription on it as Hittite or Egyptian, and kept bothering professors with this bee in his bonnet, until an archeologist happened to look at the photograph of the inscription upside down, to notice that it read, in rather cursive lettering, HECHO EN MEJICO.)

Anthropologists have blushed to see Marcel Griaule indulging in speculations about the African origins of the zodiac. The evidence is exciting, but it lacks rigor of demonstration. Yet this speculation of Griaule came to the attention of the poet Jay Wright, who knew what to do with it: namely to keep the matter where, for the nonce, it belongs, in the realm of myth and poetic imagery. Science will return to the matter when it can. The diffusionist anthropologist Leo Frobenius stirred Pound's imagination, and helped him shape *The Cantos*. Joyce had his Giambattista Vico and Giordano Bruno; Whitman had his phrenology; Joseph Cornell, that eccentric genius, stood firm upon Mary Baker Eddy. The critic assesses, and commends, the happy outcome of these processes; the scholar makes us understand them.

But the scholar, so useful as a direct source for the artist, should also inform the critic, so that he can be in full possession of his duty, which is not only to say what is best in the work of the artist, but what the artist might do next. That is, when the novel becomes long-winded and ungainly, the critic can point to the novels of Osip Mandelstam and Yuri Olesha, for their brevity and precision. Such alertings have guided the arts all along. A critic, indeed, can call things into being. Mencken bullyragged and shamed American writing out of a genteel and into a robust tradition. He defended Dreiser and Sinclair Lewis, and urged more writers to be like them, and he did this with great success. Gertrude Stein (or was it Willa Cather?) invented Hemingway and the prose of William Carlos Williams. There is a sense in which Emerson called Whitman into being.

Looking backward, it is a common thing to be able to say that there is a chain of instigations connecting poets. One such progression would be from Shelley to Browning to Pound to Zukofsky. The fragmented Greek lyric, archy and mehitabel, Jules Laforgue (by way of Eliot and Pound), and Guillaume Apollinaire converge in E. E. Cummings. Greece and China make Hilda Doolittle.

Such complexities—needing scholars to chart them—were taken for granted right up until modern education became the hodgepodge of the elective system. We are the first civilized generation to be surprised by culture. This may be a good thing. It is a kind of experimental run-through of a barbarian time in which culture only *seems* to have been lost. In the invasions of the Barbarians, texts of Cicero were used to start a fire by Mongol hordesmen who didn't know what a book was, or philosophy, or even written language. Masterpieces of art were destroyed through indifference, their beauty being imperceptible.

Solzhenitsyn, that Isaiah of our time, has asked what difference is there between Soviet suppression of the arts and American indifference to them. The difference is that between real barbarity and the experimental barbarity we have evolved. We still maintain, at probably the highest level of sophistication in the world's history, a cultural exchange system. It is wonderfully efficient. It is made up of university faculties, librarians, artists, scholars, and amiable amateurs. Once, when I was interested to write about the Soviet engineer, painter, and aeronaut Vladimir Tatlin, about whom very little is known, I knew that it was futile to ask anybody about him: for we are barbarians, and learning is scarce. I found a book about a part of Tatlin's work in the University of Kentucky Engineering Library. Ironically, the book was published in the Soviet Union, where it is sometimes available to people, sometimes not—according to which way the political wind is blowing. But some cultivated librarian had acquired the book (it is about Konstantin Tsiolkovsky, the inventor of the space rocket, as the Russians will tell you), and I became its sole reader in Kentucky. Another of my sources was a man who had known Tatlin himself—a scientist so hedged around by security that I had to wear a placard to get to his offices in Washington, where, at one point, Admiral Hyman Rickover interrupted our talk. The Museum of Modern Art has one wing of Tatlin's air-bicycle, and anybody who wants to can see it. I have recently discovered a small wooden fish that Tatlin made for a Christmas-tree ornament: it is in the Humanities Center in Austin, Texas. Our new barbarity is acquisitive—it collects anything and everything. There is something delicious in Texas oil millionaires instructing scholars to buy important things, no matter what, with the understanding that these things —manuscripts, letters, diaries, hats, socks, James Joyce's eyeglasses, Virginia Woolf's walking stick, a Soviet Christmas-tree ornament—ought to be kept. Once we collected for religious reasons, or supposed historical reasons, but now we collect in blind faith. That faith is our continuity.

If we have forgotten the past, we have not broken with it: it flows through us. We have perhaps relegated the conscious continuity of the past to the scholar, and asked the critic to keep lines of communication open between the scholar and the artist.

The modern poet who was most concerned with cultural continuities, and felt that we live in a time of cultural crisis, was Charles Olson. His own poetry is an example of the crisis he was writing about. It is difficult and allusive, and invites the scholar's attention.

I first saw Charles Olson's "The Kingfishers" in Donald Allen's epochmarking anthology *The New American Poetry 1945–1960*. This book is the critical act that ushered in the Post-Modernist Era. I was not particularly interested in the poem, as Charles Olson was only a name to me—someone who had something to do with a disreputable experimental school called Black Mountain College. Then, in 1961, the poet and publisher Jonathan Williams gave a reading at Haverford College. He read "The Kingfishers" in a rhythm and intonation which he assured us were those of the poet himself. He had studied under Olson at Black Mountain, had published the first volume of Olson's great "Maximus" suite of poems, and announced to his Haverford audience that this one poem, "The Kingfishers," was the beginning of a new order of American verse.

A year or so later, the filmmaker Stan Brakhage, himself an innovator of a new vision in cinematography, told me that "The Kingfishers" was a modern masterpiece, perhaps *the* modern masterpiece. He looked to it as a model for his arrangement of images in his films. He had sought out the poet, and had wonderful, if a bit alarming, tales of his capacity for food, drink, and conversations that lasted for days.

I then had the word of the poet Ronald Johnson, who is, in my opinion, the greatest living American poet, that "The Kingfishers" has the distinction in our time that "The Love Song of J. Alfred Prufrock" and *Hugh Selwyn Mauberley* had in theirs.

With all of this critical enforcement from poets and artists (there are more than I have mentioned; there were equally enthusiastic and equally authoritative endorsements from the film-critic P. Adams Sitney, from Jonas Mekas, and the novelist Fielding Dawson), I decided to offer a course in Post-Modernist literature, and to put "The Kingfishers" in the syllabus. William Carlos Williams had given the poem his strong approval, even though he always got the title wrong, calling it "The Bluejays"; and there was word that Ezra Pound himself had, for a while, given his stamp to Olson. They later fell out over matters political and ideological.

So the time came for me to be a step ahead of my students in a reading of this poem. I saw that the text was influenced by *The Cantos* of Pound, so that I, who had just made a study of that long poem for a doctoral dissertation, could follow the main drift of the argument, and even spot, here and there, allusions derived from Poundian sources. But there was an enormous amount of the text that would need looking up. In class I used the poem as a scholarly adventure, to show how a modern text makes demands on our knowledge. We discovered acres of ignorance in ourselves. We did what we could. I was able to locate the tradition of the poem: it was a meditation on ruins in Yucatan. Knowing the poet's book on Melville, *Call Me Ishmael*, I was able to connect the poem with "Clarel," and through it, to a family of Romantic poems, beginning with Shelley (including "Ozymandias") and persisting, as I discovered with some homework, through the *Las Altas de Machu Picchu* of Pablo Neruda, which Olson seems to have read before its masterful translation by Nathaniel Tarn (another poet, by the way, who assured me of the greatness of "The Kingfishers").

An enterprising student, as frustrated as his teacher by sections of the poem for which we could find no help at all, did something which I had neither the time nor the gall to do. He drove, one weekend, to the poet's house in Gloucester, Mass., and knocked on the poet's door. This was early on a Sunday morning. The poet, a man with a bear's physique, just under seven feet tall, had been up to a late hour. He shouted through the door that he wanted whoever was knocking on his door to desist, and go away, quickly, and forever. The student shouted through the door that he wanted to understand "The Kingfishers" and had questions about it. The poet replied that he would soon emerge, if the knocking and shouting didn't cease, and do grave damage to the head and limbs of the student. The student kept knocking. The poet bellowed. This story, implausibly, has a happy ending. The poet's rage gave way. He appeared in his clothes, in which he habitually slept, invited the student in, and told the student more about "The Kingfishers" than the student could absorb. Olson kept saying of his more cryptic allusions, "Your teacher will know what I mean."

Well, with some homework, I decoded lots of what Olson said. This heroic interview increased our knowledge of the text greatly. What Olson gave was a set of coordinates by which we could find our way through the densities of allusion. Plutarch's *Moralia* turned out to be crucial, and Prescott's *History of Mexico*, and the writings of Norbert Wiener, Marco Polo, Rimbaud, and many others.

Next, I was invited to contribute to a first scholarly study of Olson's achievement soon after the poet's death. I chose to explicate "The Kingfishers." I felt that I had a richness of resources for the parts of the poem that remained obscure. I would simply ask all the people who had commended the poem to me. Most of them knew Olson, and had the highest opinion of his status as a poet. At the very beginning of the poem, for instance, there is a description of someone named Fernand who had seen the ruins of Yucatan, and had talked about them with reference to Angkor Wat. He was someone who knew Josef Albers. All the indications pointed to Fernand being a person who had talked about kingfishers and ancient Mexican culture at Black Mountain. No trouble, there, I thought. Jonathan Williams, who had introduced me to the poem, would know who Fernand was, and all about him.

He could not, as it turned out, recall who Fernand was. He gave me the address of the poet's widow. She did not answer my letter. Fielding Dawson, who had been at Black Mountain, was able to tell me that Fernand was somebody at Black Mountain. He had heard him. He was a friend of Olson's, but who he was, and whether Fernand was a first or last name, he couldn't say. Was he, I asked, Fernand Léger, who was at Black Mountain for a short visit? Fielding Dawson didn't think so. I asked Brakhage, Ronald Johnson, others. They did not know, but could put me in touch with someone who did. These references turned out not to know, either.

In the process of trying to find out the identity of Fernand I also discovered something surprising. None of the admirers of the poem had the least notion as to the meaning of any of the allusions, obscure or otherwise.

Ronald Johnson directed my attention to the color of the words, their etymology, and beauty of diction and phrasing. But what, I asked, was "the E on the stone"? What did it have to do with Kingfishers and Mao Tse Dong? Ronald said these things didn't matter. Jonathan Williams said that I could concentrate on the energy of the poem, the freshness of the imagery, and other matters. And so it went. I very soon realized that I was as helpless as any of my students. Stan Brakhage had recited "The Kingfishers" with passion in my living room. But he had no more understanding of the poem than my cat.

I turned to more levelheaded scholars when I needed to, and got a rare hint here and there. In the end, I had to do all the work of explication just as if I were the only reader of the poem in the world, and I may well have been. I have discovered since that Ralph Maude, at Simon Fraser University, was working parallel to my research; he still is. His study, when it is published, will be better than mine, as he has tracked down drafts of the manuscript, and gone deeper into Olson's sources and instigations.

Meanwhile, I had a deadline to meet. My study was published. Without Fernand's identity. Without lots of other things. But my study gets cited as the authoritative one, though I am no Olson scholar. I simply went about the business of explication with the sense that I could not say that the poem is great until I understood it. I'm not at all certain that I do understand it. I have given a course, much later than the pioneer one, in which I have been able to show students where all the pieces of the collage come from, how the poet has transmuted them, and how most of the details interact with the tradition in which the poem was written. In this second course, a graduate one, we read not only "The Kingfishers" but all of Olson's lyric poems, discovering that the themes of the poems begin before its composition and extend far beyond. I look forward to mustering the erudition to give a course in "The Maximus Poems." In the process of explication I and my students were wonderfully improved in our education. It is not without point to observe that our research was an experience the poet may well have planned. To read the poem sensibly one has to know Heraclitus, the history of Mexico, Plutarch, geography, ornithology, Pound's *Cantos*, Albrecht Dürer's diary, archaeology, Mayan culture, Marco Polo, Rimbaud, Keats, the Bible, Shakespeare, French, and Italian. It also helps to know the geological theories of Frank Taylor and Alfred Wegener, and the subject of cybernetics as it was understood in 1948. In short, this poem, aside from all else, insists on a literacy that the 1960s seemed to be denying, and proposing to get along without.

Years afterwards, I was reading *The New Yorker*: a profile of Jean Riboud, the French industrialist and patron of the arts. The article included the information that Riboud had been a friend of Charles Olson's, whose conversation he enjoyed. They talked archaeology and history, art and aesthetics. I had found Fernand. For the record, none of the Black Mountain people to whom I turned for help had ever heard of Jean Riboud.

Now if I can find a source for the discovery of the Mongolian louse in Yucatan graves, I will have all my research in place.

The Critic as Artist

A sentence from Henry James' preface to *The Awkward Age*:

> The truth is that what a happy thought has to give depends immensely on the general turn of the mind capable of it, and on the fact that its loyal entertainer, cultivating fondly its possible relations and extensions, the bright efflorescence latent in it, but having to take other things in their order too, is terribly at the mercy of his mind.

For "happy thought" read "text." What it has to give—in exchange for attention—is its meaning. We as readers are the loyal entertainer and fond cultivator of its possible relations and extensions. But we are, in the modern period, uncomfortably aware that whereas a text used to operate in a traditional boundary, that boundary is now gone. When Milton wanted a name to have allusive force, he put it in italics. These italicized words—*Eden, Oreb, Sinai,* and *Chaos* are the ones that occur through line 10 of Book I of *Paradise Lost*—are in effect invisible footnotes, or cross-references to other texts. Sacred geography was at Milton's readers' fingertips; *chaos*—though it appears in some translations instead of "the great gulf" of Luke 16:26— would need asking about.

In the main, however, Milton's references to other texts, like those of Shakespeare and Spenser, were bounded by a fairly severe definition. They were, in any case, what the literate knew, or could easily find out. Two full streams of culture flowed from the Bible and from the Classics.

When a density of learning began to appear in English literature, there came with it the understanding that the author would teach us what we needed to know as we read along. Thus Scott is as clear and orderly a teacher of history as Shakespeare. Browning began to require a bit more attention than readers were used to. But he still feels the responsibility to teach. In such seemingly ungiving texts as "Balaustion's Adventure" and "Aristophanes' Apology," we have something like a bargain: education in exchange for close attention and patience. The reader cannot be wholly ignorant of classical literature, and yet it doesn't do him a great deal of good to be thoroughly familiar with Browning's matter—the careers of Euripides and Aristophanes, the history of their time, their theories of tragedy and comedy—for Browning is transmuting it all, and making us see it as we've never seen it before.

In moving outside the frame provided by a normal education, "Sordello" is thereby the first modern poem. It created a scandal, and many jokes about readers who thought they had lost their minds. It baffled Tennyson. It was the poem the young Pound set out to emulate when he began *The Cantos*—a text which now has a quarterly journal to explicate it, a text that was (ironically) not as obscure fifty years ago as it is now. A residuum of tolerance (and delight) remained from the Browning societies. Pound's way of seeing the Middle Ages was Browningesque.

From *The Cantos*, William Carlos Williams' *Paterson*, where the difficulty is in subtlety of technique rather than in subject matter. From *The Cantos*, Louis Zukofsky's *"A,"* where the difficulty of reading is immense, and a new kind of difficulty in any kind of poetry. From Pound's *Cantos*, the *Maximus* poems of Charles Olson.

All of these texts are difficult. The stock explanation for this is that modern life is complex: an art reflecting it must be equally complex. This insight is a bit blind, it seems to me.

It would make more sense for a complexity of life to call into being an art of great lucidity, one capable of countering confusion with clarity, one that might ascertain certainties in a chaos of uncertainty, to comfort and guide us. Indeed, that is precisely what Pound said he was doing in *The Cantos*, "cutting through the muck with clarity." If we look at the programs of the most difficult of modern writers, we will find them to be unaware, to a surprising degree, of the problems created by their work.

The most notoriously unreadable book in all English literature is Joyce's *Finnegans Wake*. Here is a sentence from it:

The horseshow magnete draws the field and don't the fillyings fly? [246]

Whatever this is, it began life as Stephen Foster's "Camptown Races." Like most of the sentences in *Finnegans Wake* (including the title) it can be sung to a tune from the great fund of childrens' songs, folksong, or opera which Joyce could count on our knowing. This appeal to common culture is crucial to understanding Joyce. *Paradise Lost* assumes precisely such a common culture, as do, let us admit, all works of art.

The *horseshow magnete* is a horseshoe magnet, and we begin to see a poetic joke: a racetrack is shaped like two horseshoes tine to tine (but if you do this with magnets, they repel each other—this is a theme all to itself, not to be pursued here). Having seen the magnet in our sentence, we see that Joyce has in mind the classroom demonstration of magnetic fields (we say "a field of horses" in a race)—iron filings poured onto a sheet of paper will arrange themselves in a pattern that makes the magnetic field visible if we hold the magnet beneath the paper.

Joyce knew that Ezra Pound, his friend and patron, had used this image—"the rose in the steel dust" Pound calls it—to claim that if Dante had known it, he would have found a way, as surely as John Donne, to use it as a valid image in poetry.

Horseshow Magnate is another meaning: a rich buyer of racehorses. And magneto. And the fillyings are fillies, and girls, and they are also *feuilles*, leaves, for the image of autumn and falling leaves is never far from Joyce's imagery.

Without its context, which is one of children staging a play for their parents in a nursery, we cannot pursue the full resonances of this sentence. The preceding sentence is "And vamp, vamp, vamp, the girls are merchand." So the girls who are fleeing the horseshow magnate are camp followers; the setting is our Civil War specifically, and all wars generally, and the battles are full of echoes of Abel and Cain, whose contention has amplified down through history into "the baffle of Whatalose when Adam Leftus and the devil took our hindmost."

I'm saying all this because I want to ask, what is the task of the critic with a text like this? First of all, we would appreciate a critic who can keep telling us that Adam Leftus was one of the founders of Trinity College, Dublin. We readers here in Virginia don't know that. A Dubliner would. French readers might appreciate a critic who can tell them about "The Camptown Races." Let's note that the best way to read *Finnegans Wake* is in a group, where one of us can sing a stanza or two of a song, after another of us has identified it. The critic blurs into the reader, the reader is made into an explicator. Joyce reinvented reading. Our own language becomes foreign for a moment. This resistance to easy understanding is one of the meanings of the book. Joyce, like most twentieth-century artists, knew that the arts were in need of being returned to their origins.

Everywhere we look in modernist writing, we can see the writer trying to get us to pay attention, to wake us from some sleep into which literacy itself has lulled us. So that the perfectly ordinary-looking opening line of Zukofsky's "A"

A round of fiddles playing Bach

cannot be read so easily once we are deep into the poem. For by that time we have come to be alert to many sets of words in which *play* and *work* dance around each other. We realize that we should have read "A round of fiddles *playing* a *work* of Bach's" and appreciated that playing the fiddle is work for musicians (who call a violin a fiddle; that should have aroused our suspicion). These musicians playing Bach are working at Carnegie Hall in 1929 (both Passover and Good Friday that year), and they are working because union fiddlers were on strike, and wouldn't play. Work, said Karl Marx, the tutelary spirit of this part of the poem (before Thomas Jefferson takes over later), should be as engrossing as play (an idea from Fourier, an evocation of whom will close the 23rd part of the poem). When Shakespeare enters the poem, and his plays, his works will begin a new playing with the word *work*.

Zukofsky eludes our reading until we learn to play with meaning as nimbly as Bottom and his mechanicals. The critic of Zukofsky has a special task of pointing. He must say, for instance, "find the horse," because a horse is concealed everywhere, like Easter eggs. Once it is so obvious that we miss it. Lost in a strange game in the 9th part of the poem—which is a translation of Guido Cavalcanti's canzone, *Una Donna mi priegha*, that keeps the metric, syllable-count, and rhymes of the Italian original, while taking its every phrase from the Everyman's translation of *Das Kapital* (a passage on work and play) and keeping the *m*'s and *n*'s in a pattern that makes a conical section on the page (a cone with a section marked being the letter *A*, another Easter egg to be found through the poem)—and appreciating the fact that this translation is meant to reply to Pound's of the same poem in *The Cantos*, and to be making a Marxist response to Pound's, we miss the horse concealed in the unnamed author being translated, Guido Cavalcanti.

Why a horse? Why the other constant images? They are the poet's wife Celia (who enters the poem as a theme in the poet's name, which ends *sky*, for which her name is the Latin *Coelia*), the letters of Bach's name, and the humble plant Liveforever, also known as houseleek, or hen-and-chickens (genus *Sedum*). We don't yet know. Scholars are working on the matter.

Zukofsky's critic, or scholar, has a very specialized task. So does Pound's, and Joyce's, and many another's. It is a peculiar feature of modern scholarship that techniques unique to the artist must be evolved for explication. The modernist scholar who has learned how to follow Proust's double images and encoded symbolism cannot transfer this expertise to a reading of *Ulysses*, for which he needs a new set of implements altogether.

This strange phenomenon may simply mean that no critic has as yet achieved a synoptic view of our time and its art. We feel a kinship among the poetic styles of Dryden, Pope, and Johnson which their contemporaries may not have felt at all.

There have always been highly individualized, eccentric styles: Aristophanes is an early example, and suggests that comedy requires sharp differentiation, as witness Rabelais, Laurence Sterne, Thomas Nashe, S. J. Perelman. Intensely personal writing demands a calm, rational normality—the great human styles of Plutarch and Montaigne, Thoreau and Colette. We would like to understand how a style, particularly in our own century, needs to be eccentric and unique. Such a style asks not for critical approval but for critical defense, so that throughout modern writing we have a writer and a critic side by side, in some kind of unplanned cooperation. The inference is that the critic is practically a subcreator, or even collaborator.

The career of the brilliant modernist critic Hugh Kenner will illustrate this phenomenon. He is the first critic to realize that twentieth-century literature is a radical break with the aesthetic direction of the nineteenth century. Hugh Kenner took his doctorate from Yale, under the guidance of the New Critics, who did not know that their skills were inadequate to deal with Pound and Joyce, but Kenner had the advantage of being an outsider—a Torontonian— and of being the protégé of that half-mad genius Herbert Marshall McLuhan, who is one of those strange figures whose brilliance can be articulated by others though not by themselves. Over the years Hugh Kenner has shown how we might read Pound, Wyndham Lewis, Joyce, Samuel Beckett, T. S. Eliot, Buckminster Fuller. These writers were being misunderstood because they do not fit into previous frames of reference; nor do they use energy systems that we are used to.

The arts in our time are integral with the world in ways that we had forgotten they can be. Pound's *Cantos* assume that they are coincidental with many historical events, as well as contemporary events, with which the poem itself does not engage. *The Waste Land* is about the First World War, a fact we have to realize. Beyond "The Fall of the House of Usher" there is no other terrain. We come to the story with the narrator, and we leave with him, never knowing where we are, or when in history we are there. Poe set up boundaries of severest demarcation, outside of which there is a void as imaginary as what's inside the boundaries. Compare this state of affairs with Beckett's *Endgame*, where the most moving consideration is for what's outside the windows. We have our suspicions that an atomic war has cancelled the world out there, or that the isolation of the four characters is so desperate that the outside world no longer exists for them.

All of Beckett—as Hugh Kenner shows—makes sense only when we locate each work in a world Beckett wants us to guess. So that when Kenner places *Waiting for Godot* in France of the Occupation, when members of the Résistance (Beckett was one) had to wait for disguised contacts who sometimes never came, he gives the play a more immediate meaning than its assumed existential one of mankind waiting for God. It is certainly that, too, as it is a philosophical comedy about all anguish of expectation, and of disappointment. Beckett himself, asked the meaning of "Godot" by one of the actors, said, "Oh, it's just me and my wife."

Pound's texts without Kenner's commentaries would be quite different, strange as it is to say so. Kenner gave us a way to read Pound, as he has given us a way to read Joyce and Beckett. This is not to say that these are the only ways to read these writers. We might note, however, that what Kenner does best is show us how to read, and how to appreciate what we read. A critic cannot hope for more success. Another Torontonian, Northrop Frye, has been equally successful in showing us a way to read Blake. The method I perceive in the successful modern critic is one of an admirable responsibility wherein the critic serves as an advocate pleading a case. There are other splendid examples: Roger Shattuck showing how Proust ought to be read, Beckett showing how Proust ought to be read.

The fine arts have required a parallel effort, and for a reason that clarifies why so much modern writing needs scholars. When painting freed itself from (or was abandoned by) patrons, paintings began to cease illustrating texts. All of Renaissance painting, for instance, refers to texts; scarcely any twentieth-century painting does. That is why we feel comfortable before very strange images in Botticelli—those men with gifts, on camels, that ox and that ass, the baby with a circle of light behind its head—and uncomfortable, and perhaps lost, before a Picasso with less strange imagery. The transition is perhaps in Goya, where he felt obliged to write on his etchings "This really happened!" or "Can you believe this?"

We can say of a text as well as a painting that it has a referential text. *Ulysses* is the most obvious example to point to, yet on reflection we discover that we can go on and on looking at poetry that assumes another text—the legends underlying Keats and Shelley and Browning; the traditional forms being reworked, such as Byron's *Don Juan*; all of Shakespeare. *The Cantos* are a collage of texts; so is the "*A*" of Zukofsky. I would go so far as to say that all modern writing is about some other text, and that this is so much the case that many writers are guardedly furtive about it, while knowing that their only hope of meaning is in our ultimately finding that other text.

Beckett's *Endgame* has four characters: Clov, Nell, Nagg, and Ham; that is, *clou*, nail, *Nagel*: *nail* in French, English, and German—three nails and a hammer, the implements for a crucifixion. All of Beckett tries to make us feel the long wait for Christ's return, which was promised "soon." There is a late prose piece of Beckett's in which the whole action is a narrator watching the hands of a wristwatch. "Monsieur Godot sends to say that he cannot come today, but will most certainly be here tomorrow." Without the text of the Gospels beneath all that Beckett has written, he does not engage with anything except an empty futility.

Flaubert's *Trois contes* are three texts over texts, and *Madame Bovary* is a transmuted *Don Quixote*. *Bouvard et Pécuchet* moves with no text beneath it, but note that it is entirely about texts (encyclopedias, manuals, and so on). So long as this is the tradition, imaginative writing implies an explainer, whether one is needed or not.

The implicit synthesis of writer and critic has sometimes gone terribly awry: there is a lesson to be learned here. During and just after the Second World War a young thief who named himself Jean Genet (the son of a prostitute, he has never known his real name) wrote several novels in prison, violent and pornographic works written with a gift for narrative and description. Various literary people admired these books, astonished as much by their naked honesty as by the romance of their being written by an authentic criminal behind bars. One of the people who got Genet out of jail was Jean-Paul Sartre, who proceeded to write a treatise on Genet's work that was longer than all his novels together. Genet read Sartre's study, and was devastated. This sympathetic study claiming so much intellect, courage, and genius for him, appalled Genet, who had never in his life read a critical book. The impact was such that Genet wrote no more novels, turning to plays instead, and hoping, we suppose, that Sartre would not write a book about them.

Another problem of author and critic is that a work of art can know things the maker of it doesn't. When I wrote an iconographic study of Grant Wood's

American Gothic, I had several complaints—one in print from Hugh Ken-ner—that I was assigning to Grant Wood knowledge he didn't have. I replied that the painting knew these things for him. Of a study I wrote of Eudora Welty, Miss Welty replied, with great kindness and friendliness, that she did not intend any of the symbolism I saw in her work. This is, let us say, daunt-ing, but again I think Miss Welty, seeing her stories in her way, which is al-ways perforce inside outwards, does not realize the extent she has kept the contours and symbols of Ovid's *Metamorphoses* (which is what I was writ-ing about) that we can see from the outside looking in.

Interpretation does not displace the artist by the critic; the critic himself is doing the placing. He is an ambassador, an advocate; in short, a helpful pres-ence. We are thankful for his studying the work of a writer and saying which is the writer's first-rate, second-rate, and third-rate work. As an ambassador for the writer, he may be free to speak directly when the writer was con-strained, or is at a cultural remove. Osip Mandelstam's *Theodosia* seems to students to be singularly pointless, plotless, and mystifying until their teacher shows them how every detail of this elegantly brief description of a Russian seaport in the time of the Civil War is meaningful. Mandelstam wrote the work with the idea that if he was clever enough, it just might get past the Soviet censors. Fifty years later, it did.

All art is symbolic to one degree or another, and the interest in a work of art is inexhaustible. We can think of interpretive studies by critics which have achieved a permanent alliance with their subjects. Martin Heidegger on Hölderlin is a critical activity happening between the poet and the philoso-pher; a professor teaching Hölderlin will not recommend it until the student proposes to write a doctoral dissertation. Other such studies are Paul Valéry on Leonardo da Vinci, Miguel de Unamuno on Cervantes, André Malraux on Goya, Linda Orr on Jules Michelet. These amount to philosophical med-itations, and descend by way of tradition from commentaries on sacred texts. Etymologically we have here pretexts, in all the senses of the word. Montaigne's long meditation on Raymond Sebond is an archetype of the form, which habitually and characteristically grows into a work of art in its own right while keeping to its pretext, its reason for existence, and its source of energy. Kierkegaard's study of *Don Giovanni* never quite elbows Mozart offstage. Even so, we are constantly aware that the center of gravity is in phi-losophy and not in music. Louis Zukofsky's study of Shakespeare, called *Bottom: On Shakespeare*, demonstrates how the search for a unifying har-mony in so large a writer as Shakespeare can involve any subject under the sun, and give the illusion that it is a universe all to itself. In this masterful work of Zukofsky's—which, as far as I can tell, Shakespeare scholars have yet to discover—we see what's meant when we discern a whole culture in one book, the way we can say that Homer is Greece, Vergil Rome, Dante the Middle Ages. English literature *is* Shakespeare, and everything the English, and English-speaking people, have written is tangent to his plays and poems.

In 1960 a technician in the Bell Telephone Laboratories discovered that he could make an image appear in a stereopticon that is neither of the two images which the stereopticon is fusing. The example I have seen is of a spatter of dots, seemingly random, in squares side by side. Through the stereopticon one sees a sharp-edged isosceles triangle beautifully defined, suspended just above the spatter of dots. This floating, Platonic triangle is nowhere but in our head. It is an authentic vision. Its visual possibility is partly in the left-hand square, partly in the right. Without the stereopticon to serve us, there is no way of discerning what latent pattern lurks in either square, realizable only in the fusion of the two.

Successful criticism, it seems to me, is like this ghostly triangle in the stereopticon. Ezra Pound here, Hugh Kenner there: and we see something we had not seen before. Professor Kenner, left to his own devices, writes about mathematics and geodesic tensegrities, or discourses on Canada or God. Ezra Pound writes poetry. Put the two together, and an unsuspected system of subjects emerges bright and clear.

This conjunction of writer and critic is apt to surprise us in larger measure than we can anticipate. Recently Ralf Norrman and Jon Haarberg, two Scandinavian critics handy with structuralist strategies, asked themselves what would emerge (by way of crystalline geometric figure floating above the spatter) if they made a survey of pumpkins, cucumbers, squash, and gourds in world literature. The result was happy, fascinating, and wonderfully surprising. They were able to write something like a formula for the iconographer to follow: that where these vegetables appear in imagery, certain meanings come with them, and certain tones are achieved. They go so far as to ask, quite seriously, if literature writes itself. Their theory approaches what we have all suspected, that culture is a language of images and ideas, and functions according to a syntax, with dialects and idiomatic constructions. If Norrman and Haarberg had chosen the rose to trace, rather than cucumbers, we could have foreseen what they would discover. The next time you have a fresh reading of Dorothy Sayers' Lord Peter Wimsey canon of novels and stories in your head, along with the four volumes of Lévi-Strauss' *Mythologies*, ask yourself what's happening in those novels when food figures in the plot. You will discover that there is a subtext of imagery in which you can discern a grammar of edibles, both poisoned and nutritive. When the critic can specify two spatter patterns, and hand us the stereopticon, to make the magic figure appear in the middle of the air, he is indeed entering the artistic process.

We have, for half a century now, been getting very good scholarly writing about the fine arts (and very poor critical writing), good scholarly work about architecture, music, film, anthropology, as well as very good scholarly writing about criticism. Most of this good writing—I am thinking of Dore Ashton and her masterful study of Balzac's *Le chef d'oeuvre inconnu* and her interpretive study of Mark Rothko; of Michel Foucault, Roland Barthes, and Lévi-Strauss himself—comes from exploring contexts with a demanding curiosity.

The universe is harmonic, or it wouldn't work. Heraclitus announced almost three thousand years ago that the harmony of the universe, that is, of everything, is hidden. The duty of philosophy is to find that harmony. Lévi-Strauss demonstrates in his study of the primitive mind that all of culture is a symbolic effort to act in harmony with the universe, its gods, demons, and weather. By extension, what we call art is this same quest, whether conducted by Rembrandt or Beethoven, Einstein or Emily Post (which two, Lévi-Strauss says, are in the same business, with table manners having a slight edge over physics in importance to culture). Seen this way, culture has as much need for the critic as for the artist. They work, to be sure, with different powers of creativity, but they work in a symbiosis.

Every writer asks us to agree to a tacit understanding of how he understands the story he is telling us. If the essence of a prose style is good manners, so is the essence of the plot. We quickly assign virtues to the writer's code of manners. When *The Pickwick Papers* swept London and soon all of England, word went around that here was a writer whose spirit was congenial, hilarious, but most of all right-minded. As it turned out with so shapeless a book, the public didn't care what Dickens wrote, so long as it had a golden quality called simply "Dickens."

Something of the same warm embrace happened to Walter Scott, and twice, first as a poet, and then as "The Author of Waverly." *Don Quixote*, *Childe Harold*, *Gone with the Wind*, *Lake Wobegon Days*—the history of publishing is rich in happy times. Walter Scott wrote his novels a chapter a day, before breakfast, and handed the chapter to the stagecoach driver before he began his other day of being a squire and judge, gentleman and scholar. Except for illness and a nasty financial snarl with his publishers later on, his career flowed along with a serenity unparalleled in literature.

Compare Joyce, writing his sentence (not chapter) a day, spending eleven years writing *Ulysses* and sixteen writing *Finnegans Wake*. The first edition of *Ulysses* was destroyed by two outraged governments (just as if the Spanish

Inquisition were still in business). Joyce made the cover of *Time* magazine when *Finnegans Wake* was published in 1939, but what the review inside said was that you can't read the book, as the text defies comprehension.

No one has ever needed a critic, or even scholar, for help in reading the Waverly novels. A comfortable chair, a fine autumn afternoon, and *Guy Mannering* or *Rob Roy*, and all is well. If a critic has written about Scott, we read him to see our delight shared by another admirer of Scott, and we are pleased to know more about Scott's matter, with the same instinct that we leave a football game in anticipation of seeing some more of it, with commentary, on TV, and to reading about it in next morning's paper.

But with Joyce we turn to critics for real help. We expect the critic to be an advocate, as well as an interpreter. We also turn to critics to help us with Shakespeare and Euripides, Dante and Dylan Thomas.

In the visual arts and in music something of the same thing has happened. We can drink in a symphony by Brahms, but with Charles Ives we ask, "What in the world does the man think he's doing?" The arts seem to have invited criticism to take up permanent residence with them.

There is also the ineluctable fact that modern artists count on interpretation by highly skilled critics, thereby giving official recognition to the symbiosis we had guessed. Louis Zukofsky is our best example here. We have so far no authoritative study of Zukofsky; all is still in the dark, where it gleams. His early work is difficult enough, his middle work grew in density, complexity, and obscurity, and his final work is, so far, perfectly impenetrable. The last book of Zukofsky's is called *80 Flowers*, a suite of eighty poems about, by golly, eighty flowers. It was printed in an edition of eighty copies, and the estate has kept it that way. There has been no reprint; none planned. Each poem has eight lines of five words, so that each poem is exactly forty words. The open book always displays, left and right, eighty words. There is no punctuation. The text at all points overlies a subtext in a language not English, and the text itself is a collage of quotation. This is close to the method of *Finnegans Wake*, but different enough to be the style of Louis Zukofsky and nobody else.

I mention this particular suite of poems because I have recently been involved with scholars working on it, and can report on their progress and their problems. Peter Quartermain, at the University of British Columbia, has made fair headway in deciphering some of the text. Prof. Alison Rieke, of the University of Cincinnati, has been working with Zukofsky's notebooks at the Humanities Center in Texas. Zukofsky kept copious notes for all of his work, and carefully deposited them in libraries. (Compare Shakespeare's apparent total disregard for his manuscripts.) These notes, in a crabbed and minute hand, are not easy to read, but they are wonderfully rewarding, as it is clear that Zukofsky wanted to provide us with all the evidence of his sources—to give us on a platter what scholars have to dig for in Joyce and Pound. He does not, however, provide a commentary on his texts, so that we're really no better off.

Last month I had letters from both Professors Quartermain and Rieke, asking me if I knew that my old tomcat Max was in *80 Flowers*. I did not. They had both found in Zukofsky's notes a letter of mine, neatly summarized, in which I had told the poet the tale of how Max's duplicitous triple existence had been discovered. Max was a white Persian tom with one blue eye and one green (the genetic arrangement whereby white Persian toms can hear, as Darwin himself discovered: two blue eyes, and they're deaf). We enticed him into our house one bitterly cold day, thinking him a stray and starving. He was very cautious about accepting the invitation; I remember that he had ice between his hairy toes, which clicked on the kitchen linoleum. He became our cat, and, like all toms, would disappear for days at a time, on business. What I had written Zukofsky was how, one Thanksgiving, we were taking an afternoon walk, and saw Max being let into a strange house, as if he lived there. Well, he did. He had lived there for years; in fact, had been born there. His name was Bunny. We met his real people, to Max's evident embarrassment, and learned that he was a very different cat at the Robinson household, preferring foods that he didn't like at our house. Some weeks after this revelation, we discovered further that Max Bunny was also the cat of a dear old lady named Nanny Montgomery, or so she thought. At her house his name was Snowball. Both these other owners of Max admitted that he was bad to go away for days at a time.

So this little neighborhood tale went into the poet's notebooks, and forms part of the poem "Thyme," where one can make out the green eye and blue eye, the seven years of his residence with us, his whiteness, the day of his being enticed in out of the cold, and other matters which I will report to the world in time, after I have decoded more of the poem. Max is in it along with Isaac D'Israeli, a rose tree, a bird, King Lear, and some other things.

What interests us here is the hermetic obscurity of the text, so far defying all readers (a predicament that has maintained in one text or another since Mallarmé), and that a poet of great talent and seriousness wrote it, and left a set of clues on deposit in a library. Should all the correspondents of the poet hold a week-long conference, with a reading from his works and from the notebooks, so that one by one we can testify to anecdotes we remember sharing with him? If my cat got into *80 Flowers*, it is very likely that Hugh Kenner's German shepherd did too: he was a particular friend of the poet's, who imagined him to be a reincarnation of St. Thomas Aquinas.

Was Zukofsky in this last book teaching us something he felt we needed to know? *Finnegans Wake* is full of instructions as to how it is to be read, and the allusions in *The Cantos* turn out to reinforce each other, so that the more we know about them, the more we see how they fit together. It is precisely this sense of field, or family, that makes modern literature different. And it is the business of the critic to be able to say where the boundaries lie, and where the center is. For the tacit agreement between writer and reader maintains— it is the order by which we can read at all—but it has undergone in our century a change whereby writing has had to insist over and over that it is, as always, words in a pattern. This pattern has always fitted, in hundreds of different ways, the pattern of the world.

In Mr. Pickwick's world you could believe that other things were happening somewhere else, in France, or in a garden down the road, but what was happening before your eyes was all that you were required to deal with. In Louis Zukofsky's world we are trying to live with the fact that an event also happens where it is known. Television allows us to experience in less than five minutes an earthquake in Mexico, a change of government in Peru, the kidnapping and assassination of hapless people in Beirut, a bank robbery in Newark, and the announcement that our government is going to collect and spend two trillion of our dollars. In and out of this we are encouraged to buy a new car, several brands of deodorant, and ersatz bacon. The telephone rings: we are hearing, by satellite, a voice from Florida or Arkansas. The newspaper, movies, magazines, radio, and TV expose other people's lives to us in an intimacy and urgency nobody on earth had experienced in times before. In fact, time and space have collapsed in on us.

At breakfast we take in, before we can shut our eyes or ears, the brutalities of a rape, a suicide, the rascality of a senator, the sex life of an evangelist. And none of this is patterned, except by the format of journalism.

Is it any wonder, then, that the arts have become so insistent on form and pattern? Or that literature seems to be guarding language possessively and protectively? Zukofsky's subject matter in his epic "A" is the family, its harmony, its privacy, its integrity. But, literature also says, there is no privacy, and no harmony, anymore. Or would say, if it could talk. Literature does not ever say anything. It shows. It makes us feel. It is, in the world's language, as inarticulate as music and painting. It is critics who can tell us what they think it means.

Balthus

Sensuous clarity, children in the old-fashioned smocks of a France only recently folded into history forever, high-ceilinged rooms, Parisian streets,
châteaux: Balthus' accomplished realism turns out on inspection to be both
lyric vision and a complex enigma.

Like his childhood mentor Rilke in the Fifth Duino Elegy he is asking who
we are in our cycle of budding, blossoming, falling to seed again *in diesem
mühsamen Nirgends.* Our "never-contented will" pitches us like acrobats
even in boredom and contemplative repose.

Rilke was meditating on Picasso's *Les Saltimbanques,* and Picasso's gesture
in buying and leaving to the Louvre Balthus' *The Children* (1937) seems a
deliberate return of Rilke's *hommage,* defining the kinship of three symbols
of *Dastehns,* the Existential *thereness.*

Balthus' adolescents are Rilke's "bees of the invisible," taking in from books,
from daydreaming, from as yet ambiguous longing, from staring out windows at trees, sustenances that will be available in time as Proustian ripe-
nesses, necessities of the heart.

Ultimately it is Balthus' sensibility that gives his canvases their distinction,
the quality of his attention, the unlikely subtlety and boldness of his sensuality, the harmony he creates of tensions, inarticulatenesses, ambiguities, volume, light, elusive moments.

Where in Greek writing you always find a running account of all the senses in intimate contact with the world, in Latin you find instead a pedantry accustomed to substituting some rhetorical convention for honest and immediate perception. Balthus has Greek wholeness.

He has the immediacy of a naive painter. Picasso's people are all actors, wearers of masks, mediators, like Picasso himself, between reality and illusion. Pierrot, woman as artist's model, the Ballet Russe, the Commedia dell' Arte dominate his entire *oeuvre*.

Nowhere in Balthus does this theme of actor and theatre appear. There is great integrity in his resisting it. His tradition stands apart from that of Rouault, Braque, Picasso, Klee, Ensor, many another for whom acting has been a metaphor and art a stage.

Nor do we find in Balthus any of the enlistments of mythology characteristic of the century. No Venuses, no Danaës, among all those girls. Even his cats and gnomes do not derive from folklore or myth. He is not part of any renaissance. His work is an invention.

Each painting is an invention, not the application of a technique. Each painting holds an imaginary conversation with some other painter, *The Window* with Bonnard, *The Farmyard* with Cézanne, *The Living Room* with Courbet, *The Dream* with Chardin.

The Mountain (in which the girl in the foreground stretches with the feline inflection of Gregor Samsa's healthy sister at the end of *The Metamorphosis*) is a dialogue with the Courbet of *Les rochers de Mouthiers* and *La falaise d'Etretat après l'orage*.

The term "modern artist" has never had a strictly temporal sense; from the beginning it has designated a totemistic clan to which one belongs according to a structure of rules with tribal overtones yet to be described. Balthus is a provisionally kin country cousin.

Sir Herbert Read, for instance, decreed that Stanley Spencer was not a modern artist. We remember that Brancusi, to please a committee, had to redraw a portrait of Joyce because it wasn't modern enough for their taste. This is like asking Shakespeare to be more Renaissance.

Balthus, I suspect, has been excluded from the clan for reasons of awesome primitiveness, and has thus remained in the distinguished category of the unclassifiable, like Wyndham Lewis, Stanley Spencer, and Lord knows who else. Modernity ended by trivializing its revolt.

Balthus and Spencer illuminate each other. Spencer's intrepid religious grounding (eccentric, Blakean, British, Bunyanesque, the naive inextricably in harmony with the sophisticated elements) is like Balthus' privileged, undisclosed, but articulate psychology.

Both painters express a sensual delight in the material world that is openly hedonistic, an accomplishment of the imagination beyond the sensitivity of criticism: the way light rakes a brick wall in Spencer, the respect for carpentry and architecture in Balthus.

Both Balthus and Spencer give us the surface of the canvas as a mimesis of natural texture, not paint. In Picasso, van Gogh, on out to the *reductio ad absurdum* of Pollack, it is paint. The difference is a philosophical one, perhaps even a religious one.

Spencer's iconography of saws, ironwork, human flesh reseen without the authority of neoclassical conventions, kettles, drying laundry, the location of shadows in naked light, parallels Balthus' return to a realism of an accomplished eye that demands accuracy of detail.

We have yet to study in modern painting the choice of motif after the break between patron and artist in the early nineteenth century. Not even the portrait as document or landscape as a sentiment for a room's decoration survives this new context for the visual arts.

This change was also a metamorphosis in taste. Malraux has his theory: that art became an absolute, that from Goya forward painting had only its authority as a witness to proceed with, alienated in one sense (from church and palace) but liberated in another to its own destiny.

Balthus' adolescents have a history. The Enlightenment, removing encrustations of convention from human nature, discovered the *durée* of childhood as the most passionate and beautiful part of a lifetime. Rousseau, Blake, Joshua Reynolds, Gainsborough, Wordsworth.

By the belle époque, children (in a pervasive, invisible revolution) had come into a world of their own for the first time in Western civilization since late antiquity, and we begin to have (in Proust, in Joyce) dramatic accounts of their world as never before.

Henry James' *The Turn of the Screw* (which now that we have Balthus seems Balthusian) is a skirmish on the border between the inner worlds of child and adult. James follows with symbols the serious misunderstanding between the interiority of the two realms.

It is significant that anthropologists around this time, inspecting other cultures, thought of themselves as studying "the childhood of mankind." Balthus is a contemporary of Gide and Henry de Montherlant who, like Fourier and Wordsworth, were trying to *place* the child's random vitality.

Balthus' adolescents in an endless afternoon of reading, playing cards, and daydreaming seem to have come, we are told, as a subject for inexhaustible meditation from *Wuthering Heights* (which he has illustrated), a dismal and hysterical novel that he reads in his own way.

What caught Balthus' imagination in it was the way in which children create a subsidiary world, an emotional island which they have the talent to *robinsoner*, to fill all the contours of. This subworld has its own time, its own weather, its own customs and morals.

The only clock I can find in Balthus is on the mantel of *The Golden Days* of the Hirshhorn, and its dial is out of the picture. Balthus' children have no past (childhood resorbs a memory that cannot yet be consulted) and no future (as a concern). They are outside time.

Modern French writing has been interested in childhood and adolescence in a way that American and English writing has not. The French see not an innocent but an experienced mind in the child. Montherlant treats children as an endangered species needing protection from parents.

Gide's understanding runs parallel, except that he makes allowance for the transformation to maturity. The child in Alain-Fournier, Proust, Colette, Cocteau inhabits a realm imaginatively animated with a genius very like that of the artist. Children live in their minds.

Baudelaire saw genius as childhood sustained and perfected. There is a sense among the French that adulthood is a falling away from the intelligence of children. We in the United States contrast child and adult as we contrast ignorance and knowledge, innocence and experience.

We do not give our children credit for having arrived at anything. They have no driver's license, no money, no sexual emotions (and are forbidden them), no real sports they can play, no power. Balthus' children are as complacent as cats and as accomplished in stillness.

We have postponed fulfillment of heart and mind far too late, so that the spiritual rhythm, or bad habit, of American children is perpetual procrastination. American writing and art make the child an actor in an adult world (Mark Twain, Salinger), not a real being in its own.

Of the autistically interior, dreaming, reading, erotic, self-sufficient child in Balthus' painting we have practically no image at all. Balthus' children are not being driven to succeed where their parents failed, or to be popular, adjusted, or a somebody.

Children are the creatures of their culture. The nakedness of human nature is clothed so soon by every culture that we are at wide variance, within and among cultures, as to what human nature might be. It was one of the hopes of our century to find out, a hope wholly dashed.

In France this question was thoroughly and originally debated during the Enlightenment and Revolution. The building facing us in *The Passage du Commerce Saint-André* was Marat's newspaper office, and the neighborhood once saw the movements of David and Diderot.

Charles Fourier concocted an elaborate philosophy to discover human nature and invented a utopian society to accommodate it, a society of children organized into hives and roving bands. Adults were, so to speak, to be recruited from the ranks of this aristocracy.

Proust's "little band" of adolescent girls at Balbec derives from Fourier, and the narrator's male presence among them is according to Fourier's plan of organization. St.-Loup and his circle constitute a Little Horde, the complement "of Spartans" to the Athenian bands.

Balthus' erotic sense disarms because of its literalness, explicitness, the evasion of vulgarity or cheapness of any sort. He brings the taste of Fragonard and Watteau into our century where it is unlikely to survive except in Balthus' careful, protective sensibility.

Watteau's ladies and milkmaids know that we are looking at them, and are forever beyond us in an imaginary world. Balthus' girls with bared crotches are usually looking at themselves, in a brown study or revery, provocative, vulnerable, neither innocent nor naive.

The girl in *The Golden Days* is looking at her fetching self in a hand mirror and is sitting so that the young man starting the fire will see her underwear, if any, when he turns. We see instead slim and charming adolescence trying on an expression for effect.

Balthus' treatment of the human figure ranges from a *gaucherie* thoroughly primitive (crones, the boy with pigeons, that cat) to a sensuality and accuracy that puts him among the master draughtsmen. He paints from inside the figure outward, as if the figure painted itself.

The psychological acumen of the portraits of Derain and Miró is Shakespearean: speaking portraits in the common lore of what a portrait should be. They are, in a disturbing sense, too lifelike. And they are not here as painters primarily, but as the fathers of daughters.

(Chagall around the time of the Derain and Miró portraits had himself photographed with his deliciously sexy twelve-year-old daughter wholly naked, achieving an *hommage* to and subtle parody of Balthus, but recognizing his authority of innovation and iconology.)

The portrait of the Vicomtesse de Noailles (1936), curiously like Wyndham Lewis' portrait of Edith Sitwell, is beguiling because of its honest, unflattering likeness and unconventionality of pose: a third-grade schoolteacher, surely, resting between classes.

This portrait illustrates as well as any of Balthus' his ability to take the bare minimum of a subject and bring it to the highest pitch of clarity, of presence. This rich spareness contrasts with the century's aesthetic of merging figure and ground in a dazzle.

The Passage du Commerce Saint-André, Balthus' masterwork, has the spaciousness and presence of a Renaissance wall painting (it is eleven feet long, ten feet high) and invites and defies a reading of its meaning as vigorously as Piero della Francesca's *The Flagellation*.

Reproductions of it trick one into believing that it is an intimist canvas, fairly small. I was unprepared for its size when I saw it first at the Centre Pompidou in an afternoon of surprises. I had just seen my first Tatlin and some late Malevitches unknown until then.

I had seen an abstraction by Ivan Puni that made me feel for the moment that western design still had everything to learn all over again from the Russians. The surprise of suddenly turning and gazing into (not *at*) Balthus' great painting was a splendid and complex emotion.

For the first time I remembered how familiar the street was to me, a locale I crossed time and again when I first knew Paris just after the war. The painting did not exist then, though Balthus must have been making studies for it, a picture to epitomize all his work.

Inside the painting's fetching mysteriousness there had been all along a familiarity that I had not isolated until I stood before the canvas itself. A more wonderful way of seeing Proust's theory of the redemption of time in triumphant proof I cannot imagine.

Another surprise was to notice that for all the resonances in this most Balthusian of all Balthus' work (the Rilkean question, as of the *Saltimbanques*, "Who are these people?", its kinship to Beckett and Sartre) it belongs with a rightness to the Paris of Simenon.

There's the same flatness and ordinariness, as if to say: Look, the world is not really a mystery at all. It appears to be, but look again. These eight people, a dog, and a doll are the very essence of a Left Bank back street. The fine strangeness of it all is in our minds.

The old woman with her cane, a concierge nipping out briefly to do her shopping, can tell you all about these people. She is the kind of spiteful old soul who gives Maigret and Janvier their best information. Seeing the painting is very like Maigret learning a neighborhood.

The figure we see from the back (a self-portrait, Jean Leymarie says in his introduction to the Skira *Balthus*), who is coming from the baker's, is a standard type in the *quartier*. Maigret would suspect him of all manner of irresponsibility, bohemian attitudes, and cosmopolitan vice.

The man at the left, resettling his trousers, and the aging dwarf on the right, are standard Simenon characters. They also belong to Beckett, a denizen of this street, whose *Molloy* and *En attendant Godot* are contemporary with the painting both in the literal and the Spenglerian sense.

These gnomish creatures, the most accessible of Balthus' enigmas, are not satiric, symbolic, or archetypal. They are simply misshapen bodies for which Balthus makes a place in order to chasten his voluptuous taste for the world. Apollo is dull without Hobgoblin.

Balthus' earlier cityscape *The Street* of 1933 (there are several versions) states with more theatricality the theme of *The Passage du Commerce Saint-André*: that pedestrians on a street are preoccupied, sealed within themselves, without cognizance of each other.

Each painting, *The Street* and the *Passage*, insists that the eye that's awake in all this sleep of attention is the artist's, making a basic definition, sweetly obvious but extraordinarily important, of what a painting is in the most archaic meaning of image, the *seen*.

We have adequate, if not accurate, reasons for the visual fields of all the epochs of graphic mimesis except the earliest and the latest. We feel confident that a Hogarth or a Goya exists in a history, an iconographic tradition, and an anthropology which we can successfully examine.

We do not have this confidence with prehistoric murals or with Balthus. We are as uncertain of Archilochos' exact meaning as of Beckett and Joyce. One pattern of meaning is lost, the other has chosen to move outside our received structure of references to enlarge it.

In the two street paintings there is first of all a sense of absurd tragedy in the discreteness of the characters. Two adolescents struggle playfully in *The Street*, unaware that they look like a rape, perhaps wholly unaware of the emotional forces disguised in their play.

The Street by Balthus, 1933.

They are like the adolescents in the roomscapes who take poses that are erotically suggestive, ambiguous, tentative of symbolism. There's the same vagueness of purposelessness in Cocteau and Proust: the love scenes between Marcel and Albertine are all purest Balthus.

These adolescents are like kittens enjoying themselves immensely at a game of disembowelling each other. Their claws are retracted; we are fairly certain that they don't know what they are doing, though nature does. What does nature know about Balthus' pedestrians on a street?

Adolescents play at sex, a cook strolls on the sidewalk, a little girl plays with a racquet and ball, a carpenter carries a plank across the street, a boy walks with a gesture like a bandleader at the head of a parade, his face rapt with inner attention and Whittingtonian aspiration.

A well-dressed woman steps onto the curb, seemingly in a revery; a mother in an apron carries a child in a sailor suit reading a handbill, as awkwardly posed as a ventriloquist's dummy. There is something of Oskar Schlemmer's lay-figure poise and plumb-line balance to them.

Indeed, if we were told that we are looking at puppets, our eye immediately supplies the strings and notices all the perpendicular lines directly above heads, wrists, and ankles that might be puppet strings visible for sections of their length: a metaphysical idea.

We remember Rilke's symbolism of puppet and angel in the *Duino Elegies*, the empty and the full, the fated and fate itself, and remember the iconography of doll, straw man, puppet in de Chirico, Eliot, Pound, Yeats, *Petroushka*, Karel Čapek, Jarry, Carrá, Ensor, Wyndham Lewis.

These sentient puppets inhabit two simultaneous worlds: they yearn (inchoate yearning applies as subject to a good half of Balthus' work) and they are "tossed and wrung" (Rilke's words in the Fifth Elegy) by fate, like the figures in Picasso's blue and rose periods.

If Balthus' figure paintings are all purgatorial in the sense that brooding, looking inward, abiding patiently for things to come are modes of existential suffering, his landscapes are his visions of paradise. Where they have figures, they are active and jubilant.

What is Balthus? The blue and rose period in color and translated from Montmartre to the Faubourgs St.-Germain and St.-Honoré? Courbet in the age of Rilke and Cocteau? He is, most certainly, the artist whose vision of the French spirit will increase in subtlety and radiance.

Nabokov's Don Quixote

"I remember with delight," Vladimir Nabokov said in 1966 to Herbert Gold, who had travelled to Montreux to interview him, "tearing apart *Don Quixote*, a cruel and crude old book, before six hundred students in Memorial Hall, much to the horror and embarrassment of some of my more conservative colleagues." Tear it apart he did, for good critical reasons, but he also put it back together. Cervantes' masterpiece was not in Nabokov's syllabus at Cornell, he was apparently not fond of it, and when he began preparing his Harvard lectures on it (Harvard having insisted that he not omit it) his first discovery was that American professors had over the years gentrified the cruel and crude old book into a genteel and whimsical myth about appearance and reality. So first of all he had to find the text for his students under all the prissy humbug a long tradition of misreading had sifted over it. Nabokov's new reading is an event in modern criticism.

Nabokov's intention to polish these lectures given at Harvard in 1951–1952 and at Cornell from 1948 to 1959 was never realized, and those of us who were not among "the 600 young strangers" enrolled in Humanities 2 at Harvard, spring semester 1951–1952, must read Nabokov on Cervantes from notes that survived in manila folders, scrupulously and splendidly edited by Fredson Bowers, the most distinguished of American bibliographers.[1]

Memorial Hall, where Nabokov read these lectures, is as symbolic a place for them as the most fastidious ironist could wish. It is a gaudy Victorian pile

[1] Vladimir Nabokov, *Lectures on Don Quixote* (New York: Harcourt Brace Jovanovich, 1983).

that Mark Twain's Connecticut Yankee could assure us is precisely the bamboozled composite of mediaeval architecture he saw in his dream. It was designed as a pilot example of Collegiate Gothic in 1878 by William Robert Ware and Henry Van Brunt, to memorialize the soldiers slain by quixotic Confederates in the Civil War. In this building precipitated from the imagination of Sir Walter Scott and John Ruskin, in this consummately quixotic architectural rhetoric, what could be more fitting than that a connoisseur of ridiculous postures and keen nuances should jolt us awake in the matter of the ingenuous old gentleman from La Mancha.

Once, when I was teaching *Don Quixote* at the University of Kentucky, a student raised his long Baptist arm to say that he had come to the conclusion that the hero of our book is crazy. That, I said, is something that has been discussed for four hundred years and now we, snug in this classroom on an autumn afternoon, get to have our shot at it. "Well," he muttered with some querulousness, "I find it hard to believe that they would write a whole book about a crazy man." His *they* is correct. The book Nabokov took apart so deftly at Harvard was a book evolved from Cervantes' text, so that when one brings up *Don Quixote* in any discussion, the problem of whose Quixote arises. Michelet's? Miguel de Unamuno's? Joseph Wood Krutch's? For Cervantes' character, like Hamlet, Sherlock Holmes, and Robinson Crusoe, began to stray from his book almost as soon as he was invented.

Not only has there been a steady sentimentalization of the Don and his sidekick, Sancho Panza—sweet, charmingly befuddled Don Quixote! comic Sancho, so picturesquely a levelheaded peasant!—but a displacement as well of the text by its illustrators, especially Gustave Doré, Honoré Daumier (and nowadays Picasso and Dalí), its celebrators, imitators, dramatizers, and users of the word *quixotic*, which means anything you want it to mean. It should mean something like *hallucinated*, *self-hypnotized*, or *play in collision with reality*. How it came to mean *admirably idealistic* is an explanation Nabokov undertakes in these lectures.

To put Cervantes' Don Quixote back into Cervantes' text, Nabokov (en couraged by the need to do so after looking into a batch of American critics and their laughably irresponsible accounts of the book) first wrote out a chapter-by-chapter summary—which Professor Bowers helpfully includes. The diligence of this summary can only shame those teachers who still have a week's go at *Don Quixote* in sophomore survey courses all over the Republic without having read the book since they themselves were sophomores, without ever having read Part II, or (I know of one) not having read the book at all. For *Don Quixote*, as Nabokov knew with some pain and annoyance, is not the book people think it is. Far too many interpolated *novelle* (of the kind we cheerfully forget mar *The Pickwick Papers*) impede the plotless plot. We all rewrite the book in our heads so that it is a picaresque succession of events: the appropriation of the barber's basin as Mambrino's helmet, the tilt at the windmills (which became the quintessence of the book), charging the sheep, and so on. Many people wholly innocent of the text can supply you with a plausible plot summary.

What Nabokov's eyes kept seeing as he prepared his lectures was the accurately perceived fact that the book elicits cruel laughter. Cervantes' old man who had read himself into insanity and his smelly squire were created to be the butt of mockery. Quite early readers and critics began to sidestep this Spanish fun and to interpret the story as another kind of satire: one in which an essentially sane, humane soul in a crass and unromantic world can only appear as insane.

The problem is not simple. Spain, which has traditionally rejected outsiders, has no talent (like China or the USA, for example) for accommodating them. In Cervantes' lifetime there was the hysterical expulsion of Jews, Moors, and converts of Jewish and Islamic origins. Spain kept the gladiatorial slaughters in an arena (for the amusement of the populace) long after all the rest of the Roman Empire had abandoned them. The national entertainment, the bullfight, sets Spain aside among civilized people even today. The historical moment in which *Don Quixote* was written, the reign of Felipe II, that paranoid fanatic who styled himself the Most Catholic King, is one we have silvered over with a moonlight of Romance. Nabokov was lecturing in the hotbed of Spanish romanticizing. Lowell and Longfellow had invented a Spain which has stuck in the American imagination (as witness the musical *Man from La Mancha*) and which, pitifully, American tourists flock to Spain to find.

And yet, in its way, the Spain of Felipe II was quixotic. Its nobles owned suits of armor in which no cavalryman would dare to try to conduct a battle. Felipe, practical nattering fussbudget of a king, used to stand his empty suit of armor at attention to review his troops. He himself was inside the palace, among his voluptuous Titians, doing the accounts, reading and annotating every letter sent and received in his network of embassies and spies as wide as from the New World to Vienna, as deep as from Rotterdam to Gibraltar. He, if any model is to be found, is Don Quixote, but an anti-Quixote. Like the Don, he lived in a dream whose illusory fabric kept tearing. He burnt heretics, but how do you know a heretic is a heretic? Was he not in the same epistemological hot spot as Don Quixote seeing sheep as sheep but also as Moors? Felipe's cruel spies were forever hauling people who said they were good Catholics to the torturer on the suspicion that they were (if you knew how to find out) insincere converts, Humanists, Protestants, Jews, Muslims, atheists, witches, or God knows what.

Europe was going through a time in which reality began to flip-flop. Hamlet teased Polonius with the ambiguous shapes of clouds. Don Quixote's abilities to fool himself are a focus of the age's anxieties. Identity, for the first time in European history, became a matter of opinion or of conviction. Chaucer's laughter at "pigges bones" was not skepticism of authentic relics to be venerated. But in *Don Quixote* the confusion of a horse trough with a baptismal font seriously opens the question (whether Cervantes intended to or not) as to whether what we call a baptismal font isn't a water trough innocent of all the quixotic magic we assign to it.

Over the years, I think, the meaning of *Don Quixote* has skewed into the winds of the Enlightenment and sailed brightly under false colors which we have all too willingly wished upon it. This is what brought Nabokov's gaze into such stringency. He wanted the book to be itself alone, to be a fairy tale, to be an imaginative construct independent of the myth "real life." And yet *Don Quixote* is precisely a book that plays games with "real life." In its way it is a kind of treatise about how meaning gets into things and lives. It is a book about enchantment, the inappropriateness of enchantment in a disenchanted world, and the silliness of enchantment in general. Despite this, it enchants. It became, with much misreading and cooperation on our part, what it mocked.

Nabokov, astute observer of the American psyche, knew that all six hundred Harvardlings and Cliffies in his audience believed in knights, just as they believed in the Old West with its cowboys errant, and in the Gothic architecture of Memorial Hall. He wasted no time disabusing them; in fact, cheerfully told them they would hear nothing of Cervantes, his times, or his missing left hand (lost at Lepanto) from *him*. Instead, he insisted that they know what a windmill was, and drew them one on a blackboard, and instructed them in the names of its parts. He told them why a country gentleman might mistake them for giants—they were an innovation in seventeenth-century Spain, the last country to hear of anything new in all Europe.

He is very clear, and very funny, about Dulcinea del Toboso. But he does not scatter his students' attention by digressing on Courtly Love, its strange metamorphic history, and its curious survival today. If, as he delivered these carefully wrought revisionist lectures, part of his mind was surely over at the University Museum four minutes walk away, where he spent eight years of the preceding decade as research fellow in entomology studying the anatomy of butterflies, another part must have been on a project concerning

Courtly Love, its madnesses and follies, which would mature three years hence as *Lolita*. That diminutive of a Spanish name, Dolores, raises our curiosity. *Lolita* is too logically a progression of Nabokovian themes (the other as the self, the generative power of delusions, the interplay of sense and obsession) to have been influenced by a close and tedious reading of the *Quixote*. And yet there's the picaresque journey as the "harmonizing intuition" of the two works. And there's the sprite Lolita. She began as a seductive child in the first appearance of romantic love in the West, boy or girl, Sappho's darlings or Anakreon's striplings. Plato philosophized these hopeless loves into something called the love of Ideal Beauty. The theme became salacious and overbearing in the leaden hands of the Romans, melted almost away in the early Middle Ages, to emerge again in the tenth century as Romance. By Cervantes' time Courtly Love had saturated literature (it still does), and in his satire of it and of its new context Chivalry, he found it obvious enough to transmute the stock paragon of virtue and beauty into a country girl with big feet and a prominent wart.

Don Quixote had no effect whatsoever on the health of the Romance; it simply invented a robust and parallel tradition which has moved alongside ever since. A Richardson would now have a Fielding. We would keep the ideal beauty, but in the house next door lives Madame Bovary. Scarlet O'-Hara and Molly Bloom, spirited Irish women both, have equal claim on our imagination. Even in the old romances, from early on, the virtuous beauty is balanced by a sorceress, Una by Duessa. After *Don Quixote* the false beauty began to be interesting in herself, an Eve claiming her old prerogatives as temptress. By the late seventeenth and eighteenth centuries she had set up shop both in literature and real life. To get at a French king, Michelet observed, you had to wiggle your way through a wall of women. The mistress became a kind of social institution; literature said she was demanding and dangerous, but more interesting and gratifying than a wife, a ritual detail of the Romance *Don Quixote* supposedly laid by the heels. In the overripe Decadence the mistress became a spicy Lilith, the primeval feminine in a lacy nightie, reeking of doom, damnation, and death. Lulu, Benjamin Franklin Wedekind called her. Molly, said Joyce. Circe, said Pound. Odette, said Proust. And out of this chorus Nabokov plucked his Lulu, Lolita, whose real name was more Swinburnian, Dolores, blending her with her cousins Alice (Nabokov is the translator of *Alice in Wonderland* into Russian), Ruskin's Rose, and Poe's Annabel Lee. But her Grandmama was Dulcinea del Toboso. And Humbert Humbert's memoirs, we remember, are offered to us by a professor as the ravings of a madman.

So these lectures are not without their interest to admirers of Nabokov's novels. Both Cervantes and Nabokov recognize that playing can extend beyond childhood not as its natural transformation into daydreaming (which psychiatrists find so suspicious, and discourage) or creativity of all sorts, but as play itself. That's what Don Quixote is doing: playing knight-errant. Lolita's side of her affair with Humbert Humbert is play (she is surprised that grown-ups are interested in sex, which to her is just another game), and the psychology of Humbert (meant to elude the theories of Freud) may be that he is simply stuck in the playtime of childhood. In any case, whenever a critic considers the picaresque novel, or literary treatments of illusion and identity, he will find himself thinking of Cervantes and Nabokov together.

These lectures on Cervantes were a triumph for Nabokov in that I think he surprised himself in his final opinion of *Don Quixote*. He approached his task conscientiously despite thinking of this old wheeze of a classic as a white elephant and something of a fraud. It was the suspicion of fraud that propelled his interest. Then, I think, he saw that the fraud was in the book's reputation and epidemic among its critics. Here was a state of affairs that Nabokov liked to go at *bec et ongle*. He began to find symmetry, of sorts, in the sprawling mess. He begins to suspect that Cervantes is unaware of the book's "disgusting cruelty." He begins to like the Don's dry humor, his engaging pedantry. He accepts the "interesting phenomenon" that Cervantes created a character greater than the book from which he has wandered—into art, into philosophy, into political symbolism, into the folklore of the literate.

Don Quixote remains a crude old book full of peculiarly Spanish cruelty, pitiless cruelty that baits an old man who plays like a child into his dotage. It was written in an age when dwarfs and the afflicted were laughed at, when pride and haughtiness were more arrogant than ever before or since, when dissenters from official thought were burnt alive in city squares to general applause, when mercy and kindness seem to have been banished. Indeed, the first readers of the book laughed heartily at its cruelty. Yet the world soon found other ways of reading it. It gave birth to the modern novel all over Europe. Fielding, Smollett, Gogol, Dostoevski, Daudet, Flaubert shaped this fable out of Spain to their own ends. A character who started out in his creator's hands as a buffoon has turned out in the course of history to be a saint. And even Nabokov, always quick to detect and expose the cruelty at the core of all sentimentality, lets him have his way. "We do not laugh at him any longer," he concludes. "His blazon is pity, his banner is beauty. He stands for everything that is gentle, forlorn, pure, unselfish, and gallant."

In That
Awful Civil War

The Johnson Boys were boys of honor,
They knew how to court the maids,
They knew how to hug and kiss!
Hop up, pretty girls, don't be afraid!
Hop up, pretty girls, don't be afraid!

They were lads of skill and courage,
And their side was very far,
And they joined the country's service
In that awful Civil War.
Hop up, pretty girls, don't be afraid!
                                    "The Johnson Boys"

Abbvill District South Carolina, runs a family document I have before me, *I Wᵐ⁰ Wair of Abbvill District recived of J. J. Mattison Nine Hundred Dollars it in full being for a Negro boy named Brister about 18 years old for which I warnt to be sound in boddy and mind, and free from the clames of any person or person's whatsoever in witness whear of I set my hand and seal December 17ᵗʰ. 1855 Wᵐ⁰ Wair, Test by Daniel Mattison.* This J. J. Mattison was my great-grandfather. This past May, a member of the American Academy and Institute of Arts and Letters scribbled a note and passed it over to me while that distinguished organization was dispensing its annual bounty of prizes and medals. The sender, hearing that I was born in Anderson, South Carolina, informed me, as a point of interest, that his family had once resided in Abbeville, just down the road. So whatever the fate of the slave Brister whose body my family had bought for $900, he most certainly would have known the great-grandparents of the man who slipped me the note, who was Ralph Ellison.

The reverberations of the Civil War will chime through our lives for a long time yet. We are still very much in its aftermath. Except for Vietnam (against the horrors of which we have achieved a self-induced amnesia), all our wars are over, dismissed from our concern, all but the hideous war that raged along the Mississippi and in the Virginia hills for four terrible years. If, at a public ceremony, my birthplace were given as Picardy, Burma, Anzio, or San Juan, who would scribble a note to say that his grandparents once lived nearby, and pass it over?

If the past is prologue, it is also a record of grievances to call up and enlist as excuses. All you need is rhetorical talent and a gift for rationalizing. History is also a wardrobe of costumes. The Confederacy, as Mary Chesnut demonstrates on every page of her Civil War diary, was born dressing up in a gaudily eclectic array of costumes.[1] Mark Twain blamed the Civil War on Sir Walter Scott. We see the truth of his whimsy. Beauregard was a marshal of Napoleon, soldiers were *chevaliers* from the Middle Ages, statesmen were Greek and Roman orators (who had of course owned slaves), the Confederacy was the Scots Highlands with its fearless and patriotic clans. Every Adonis of a lieutenant was Lord Byron at Missolonghi. Mary Boykin Chesnut's diary begins with Secession, and she rapidly turns from the roomfuls of senators and judges and hysterical women which she describes so well to the Scottish poet Campbell:

> Their bosoms they bared to the glorious strife
> And their oaths were recorded on high
> To prevail in the cause that was dearer than life
> Or crushed in its ruins to die.

She keeps this interplay between reality and myth for some seven hundred pages: ". . . at supper at the Haynes', Wigfall was sent for to address a crowd before the Mills House piazza. Like Fitz James—when he visits Clan Alpine again—it is to be in the saddle, &c&c. So let Washington beware." As a refined lady she did not actually hear Senator Wigfall's speech to the vulgar crowd in which he announced the inevitability of war with the North and promised to return to the Washington he had left in the saddle, with naked sabre, triumphant. Such things were conveyed to her over "pâté de foie gras,

[1] *Mary Chesnut's Civil War*, edited by C. Vann Woodward (New Haven: Yale University Press, 1981).

salad, biscuit glacé, and champaigne frappé," a supper which she found "a consolation." This supper, as we must supply with our imagination, was prepared and served by slaves who kept their own counsel.

During the bombardment of Fort Sumter, Mary Chesnut notes that the slaves were uncommonly silent as they went about their work, giving no sign that they heard the cannon, or that they were aware of their significance.

Mary Boykin Chesnut (1823–1886), the wife of a South Carolina plantation owner, politician, and founder of the Confederacy, was as fine a specimen of her type as you can come up with. The Boykins were in Virginia in the seventeenth century, and in South Carolina before the Revolution. They were all Somebody. She was educated at a French girl's school in Charleston, visited the frontier in Mississippi as a girl (a bad experience that caused her to begin to doubt the morality of slavery, of which she was outspokenly critical—but we must remember that bookish, cultivated women were made allowances for, and not taken seriously). She married well. She knew everybody. Her information about what was happening in the world came from senators, generals, Mrs. Jeff Davis. She prodded her husband into greater ambition; he was "too High South Carolina" for his own good. She was childless. She had considerable literary talent, wrote unpublishable novels, and eventually satisfied her longing to write something readable and memorable by spending the end of her days working up her sketchy Civil War diary into the skillfully wrought artifact that has come down to us, and which Prof. C. Vann Woodward has edited definitively with great care and painstaking scholarship.

The diary has a history of its own. It was first published in 1905, edited by Isabella Martin and Myrta Lockett Avary, as *A Diary from Dixie*. The editors took liberties with the text (suppressing, for example, a murder in the family). This edition, with more liberties taken, was reissued by the novelist Ben Ames Williams in 1949. Both these texts, as Prof. Woodward points out, are made to adhere to received notions of the myth of the Old South, for which, I suppose, Margaret Mitchell must be recognized as the official mythmaker.

It was Ben Ames Williams' romanticized text that Edmund Wilson made on over in *Patriotic Gore*, praising it for its uncanny awareness of historical moment and for its novelistic qualities. Both Williams and Wilson were unaware that they were talking about a conscious work of art written twenty years after the time it purported to record day by day. Enough of the original sketch diary remains for us to see how well Mrs. Chesnut forged the 1880 version. Severe critics have called the text as we now have it a fraud, but I know of no law against working up one's diary for publication.

I began reading this diary ill-disposed to put up with it. For one thing, the voice. It is the voice of all the insufferable prigs in the South then and now. It is the voice, with its muscovados triphthongs and Master Race *hauteur* that I heard quite enough of in a South Carolina upbringing ("But you *hayev* dad-mit a nigra baby is jess the cutest lil ole *thang*") and which can no longer free itself from instant caricature: "Fote Sumtah'z bin fod upon mah rejmunt leaves t'morra." We are no sooner into the diary than Mrs. Chesnut tells us she suffers from not being able to enter a room without all the gallant gentle-men (her word, not mine) falling in love with her. She discusses the gallantry (her word) of duelling with the coolness of a Regency Corinthian. Her soci-ety took it for granted that one Christian gentleman would cut another to death with a bowie knife, while himself being cut to death with a bowie knife, if one of them had cast an aspersion on one of their female kin, or on their manner of dealing cards, or on the genetic components of their ances-try.

One gets used to her voice, however, for it is one of variety and intelligence. She is aware of the narrowness of her times, she thinks ("Who is more a slave than a wife?"), she is sympathetic, critical, wonderfully observant. If she is comically a woman of her period, trained in pettiness, gossip, whining, and all the wiles and fripperies for which Confederate women are famous, that is not her fault. If these emblems of type were not hers, she would have been the wrong woman to write the dramatic, richly detailed narrative she has left us. It is a book you can open anywhere for a good hour's reading. You will find more characters than in Tolstoy, good dialogue, good waspy gossip— the Civil War day by day as it was known to people in crinoline and alpaca in Victorian rooms, French novels on rosewood tables. "Oranges are five dollars apiece." It is remarked upon that Stonewall Jackson is "a blue-light Calvinist" and thus does not have the comfort of being able to cuss like a man. Young men in yellow gloves and with names like Barnwell Rhett, Jr. and St. Julien Ravenel kneel and kiss one's hand before riding off to be slain in a glory of bugles at Chickamauga.

To read Mary Chesnut, as I did, in the same month as William McFeely's *Grant* [2] is not only to see the Civil War from the opposite side, but also on the battlefields as distinct from the Southern parlor, and from a masculine and Stoic point of view rather than a feminine and emotional one.

[2]William S. McFeely, *Grant: A Biography* (New York: Norton, 1981).

Prof. McFeely has written a traditional biography of Grant that is also an historical essay about nineteenth century American men (in transition between the frontier experience and the world of the technocrat and financial manager they had nothing significant to do), war, and the presidency. He traces the young Grant's all but aimless drift from rural Ohio to West Point (one way to get out of a small town and a lifetime of tanning leather alongside his father). Timidly he allowed his congressman's mistake for his name, Ulysses Simpson Grant, to replace the Hiram Ulysses Grant of the birth register. It is a surprise to learn that he was interested in literature and painting in oils, at which he was good.

He has come down to us in the popular imagination as a dullard who drank and a president who may or may not have noticed corruption in his cabinet. He is our Honest Soldier, taciturn, blunt, and humorless. Yet his *Memoirs*, written at the very end of his life (Mark Twain urging him on), have been admired (Gertrude Stein being among the admirers) for their Roman clarity. Indeed, Grant can easily be seen as a figure in Plutarch. He was never out of character. Even his foibles and tragic weaknesses were thoroughly consistent with the way he thought. His moment to be truly great came in the Reconstruction, when he could have sent in the army to help Adelbert Ames, the carpetbagger governor of Mississippi and one of the most good-hearted, well-meaning Liberals in American history. Ames was, in his idealistic way, within sight of establishing equal rights for freed slaves and of introducing democracy to a feudal society. The Ku Klux Klan and other murderous bullies blocked his way. He appealed to Grant, whose opinion it was that the South had seen all it could stand of the U.S. Army. Grant's own scheme was to settle American blacks in Santo Domingo, which would be a state all their own. No one in the government, or in Santo Domingo, could ever see what Grant expected to come of this plan, which had only an elementary simplicity to recommend it.

Grant began his career with a series of failures as a businessman. The Mexican War showed him his destiny. When the Civil War began, he blundered up the ranks battle after bloody battle. His idea of war was that you killed the enemy. When you had killed all of the enemy, the war would be over. McFeely's descriptions of battle are horrifying and unremittingly realistic. He stylizes nothing, romanticizes nothing. In all of Douglas Southall Freeman's *Lee's Lieutenants* you get nothing like the description McFeely gives of the cowards huddled along the banks of the river at Shiloh, or of the pig-sticking cruelty of the Confederate attack before dawn, when the Northern regiments were naked in their bedrolls. (In two days at Shiloh more men died than in the Revolution, the War of 1812, and the Mexican War altogether.)

The Civil War was, as Sherman said in Ohio the year that Mrs. Chesnut began to rewrite her diary, "all hell." And Grant pushed through it doggedly, drunk, sending his laconic telegrams, sparing nothing. He was apparently without ideals (he owned five slaves when the war began), without a shred of romance or religion (he was baptized a few days before he died). He was simply a soldier; to win a war you kill the enemy. Some of his battles were the worst planned and most cruelly executed in military history.

He was an indifferent president, missing greatness chance after chance. In one sense he freed the slaves and slovenly allowed them to be enslaved again to bigotry, poverty, and prejudice. (But then Eisenhower, as president of Columbia, did not think it appropriate that there should be a black guest at a banquet over which he was to preside.) His presidency was scandal all the way through. Then he went round the world, God knows why. He rarely made a speech over five sentences long. At the opera he was apt to rise in the middle of the overture, and say, "Well, we've heard about enough of this, haven't we?" To visit Bismarck in Berlin, he walked over to the palace and knocked on the door, the way he called on his cabinet members when he was president. He was, in his ornamentless blue uniform, his scuffed boots, and the cavalry hat so hopelessly inelegant in the Brady photographs, destiny itself.

The first value of history is that we can see the war at Mary Chesnut's side, and at Grant's, and know the man (as she could not) who took Lee's sword at Appomattox. History must be human before it can give up any meaning at all. McFeely is a biographer of great compassion. Anyone who really wants to know the history of the American black's misery should read his account of the first black cadet at West Point, during Grant's administration. He was heckled and hazed as pitilessly as any Jew at Auschwitz, and one of his chief tormentors was Grant's son. The black, James Webster Smith, of South Carolina, survived his persecution, only to be flunked by a philosophy professor.

No one imagines, a century and a half later, that any of this is over. This summer also saw the publication of one of the sharp-eyed overviews of slavery ten years before the war, Frederick Law Olmsted's newspaper reports of a long trip through the southern states—ostensibly a study of agriculture and the economic effectiveness of slave labor, but in reality a sensitive sociological assessment of plantation and city culture.[3] Olmsted, later a parks de-signer and conservationist, was at this time a newspaperman close to Parke Godwin, Edward Everett Hale, and other Liberals. His account of the Old South triangulates with Mrs. Chesnut and McFeely to show us the actual structure and feel of slavery. The system was, as even the plantationers were quick to admit, ridiculously inefficient. Olmsted kept running into pleasant, bumble-brained slaveholders who complained that the slaves were driving them crazy with their shiftlessness, overbreeding, and irresponsibility. They opine that they would be grateful if the North would free them.

But by that time the South was caught in a trap of its own making. Even if, like Jefferson, Southerners were willing to free the slaves, what would these childlike creatures do? (This argument conceals the terrible fear of the slaves' retribution, and of their being a permanent reminder of the inhumanity that enslaved them.) A battery of arguments was always trundled out for Olmsted: Northern wage earners in New England were worse fed and housed than the slaves, and English slum dwellers were infinitely worse off. The slaves were better off than in Africa, where they had been enslaved by their own people. And so on.

Olmsted's South is a South Mrs. Chesnut probably was aware of but with-out Olmsted's perspective. It was shoddy, run-down, everything in ill repair. The neoclassical mansions were beautiful, but ringed with slave-cabins (close enough to keep an eye on—I hadn't suspected this) they lost a great deal of their charm. Most slave owners complained of being pestered out of their minds by slaves who, forbidden initiative and treated like idiots, always liked to ask if something were all right before doing it.

What Olmsted shows us is a culture in the raw, capable of a high civiliza-tion in Charleston drawing rooms and in a few private homes, but for the most not working, clumsy, perhaps purposeless to those who took stock of what they thought they were doing. In their most idealistic picture of them-selves, Southerners looked back to Greece and Rome (a decade or so after the century of the Enlightenment!) for a model, but many of them must have seen that they were awkwardly out of phase, that they were maintaining a feudal society in the dawn of the Age of Steam. Slavery gave them the oppor-tunity to be idle, demoralized, and vain. The beautiful irony is that it was a man bored with being idle, for whom the war was something to do, who

[3] *The Papers of Frederick Law Olmsted*, edited by Charles Capen McLaughlin, Volume II: *Slav-ery and the South* 1852–1857, edited by Charles E. Beveridge, Charles Capen McLaughlin, and David Schuyler (Baltimore: Johns Hopkins University Press, 1981).

fought them to the death over an ideal which perhaps both North and South, each in its own way, had betrayed.

Whether the war accomplished anything that political evolution would not have achieved in time is a question with many answers. It was so complex a war that it can be said to have begun before the Republic itself, and to be still going on.

More Genteel than God

Noah Webster's last words, "The room is growing crepuscular," put the old codger before us in a fine light. Pedantically genteel, they were worthy of the schoolmaster whose *A Grammatical Institute of the English Language* (known to schoolteachers from Maine to Georgia as "Webster's Blue Back Speller") had sold in millions—and is still in print—and whose *An American Dictionary of the English Language* was the Republic's absolute arbiter of spelling and usage. In one of its two hefty volumes his grieving but puzzled family found the meaning of "crepuscular."

Richard M. Rollins' study[1] of Webster is an essay in the history of ideas rather than a biography, and has something of the air of discovery about it, as if he hadn't suspected Webster of being so curmudgeonly a reactionary, so sanctimonious a fundamentalist, or so smug a pessimist. Rollins keeps Webster well-placed against his historical background; so much so, in fact, that Webster disappears into it. We lose sight of him in the panorama. This is a tactical error, for practically all readers will be familiar enough with the history of Webster's time, whereas Webster himself is one of those figures we think we know something about, but don't. His family, his trips to Europe, his everyday behavior, his scientific interests, his manner in the classroom— our curiosity in all these matters is disappointed while we are taken through pages of squabblings between Federalists and Republicans.

The official biography of Webster enshrined in the front of the Merriam-*Webster's Third International Unabridged* is a masterpiece of euphemism.

[1]Richard M. Rollins, *The Long Journey of Noah Webster* (Philadelphia: Univ. of Pennsylvania Press, 1980).

The truth is that Webster did not believe in democracy. It had been ruined, he was convinced, by the vote, scoundrels in office, atheists (Thomas Jefferson, for example), sin, drink, and general mumpery. "We deserve all our public evils. We are a degenerate and wicked people." He believed in the literal truth of the Bible but disapproved of its coarseness, and he politely reworded its sacred text so that its blunt way with anatomy, reproduction, and heroic odors would not offend New England sensibilities. Isaiah would have thought him a prig. He was the sort of man who in Heaven would think himself too good to associate with a salacious wop like Dante.

The *Dictionary* is a doughty deed: seventy thousand entries, twenty-five years' labor, and the last comprehensive dictionary to be compiled by one man. Samuel Johnson's great opus had been *the* dictionary for seventy-three years when Webster published his. In the meantime technology had proliferated, America had spawned new words prodigiously, and the science of linguistics had made its appearance. Webster, however, paid scant attention to new American words and turned a blind eye to linguistics. He was committed to his fundamentalist theory that the Ur-language was Chaldee as spoken by Adam, Eve, and God. All other languages came from the confusion at Babel. Webster's etymologies are therefore naively wrongheaded when they are not downright wrong. "Webster," said Sir James Murray, the first editor of the *Oxford English Dictionary*, "had the notion that derivations can be elaborated from one's own consciousness."

It was typically American, this homemade dictionary. Like Franklin in science and Fenimore Cooper in the novel, Webster drew on a heroic New World *virtù*, and was given credit for this prodigious work here and abroad as an achievement of universal erudition and the purest of morals. He himself thought of it as a conservative bulwark against the tide of Jacobinism, vulgarity, and ungodliness which he felt was washing away the foundations of the young republic. Something had to hold fast. He chose to defend, purify, and set in order the one common social bond, language. If enough people wrote and spoke with a nice regard for the accurate meanings of words, all might not be lost. Webster felt that truth was in words—is not language a divine gift?—and that we owe them reverence. He hoped to lead us away from the mischief of cant and the sloth of vagueness. Not law, religion, or literature can speak meaningfully with imprecise words.

A lexicographer has godlike powers. Everything in the world passes his gaze and inspection. He can, like Johnson, define *Pope* as "the bishop of Rome," in grand dismissal of the word, or *whig* as "a faction." He can omit noisome words, ride his hobbies (Webster defined *democrat* as "synonymous with the word Jacobian [*sic*] in France"), and play not only tyrant but God himself creating the world. It is thanks to Webster's insistence on pronouncing vigorously and fully that we today mispronounce *falcon*, *clapboard*, *forehead*, *cemetery*, *often*, and many another word Americanized by being divided up into syllables in the Blue Back Speller. Rollins' discussion of Webster the lexicographer is the best part of his study; he might plausibly have built his book around the *Dictionary* rather than around Webster's about-face disillusionment with the American experiment. The one touched everybody and has continued to be a shaping force; the other was forgotten (like Patrick Henry's disgust with the young country, or Cooper's reservations about democracy).

We still say "light and dark meat" to satisfy Webster's prudery, avoiding the depraving words *breast* and *thigh*, and *limb* instead of the suggestive *leg*. It is perhaps a clue to sociological tensions between classes that Webster's high-minded vocabulary exerted moral sanctions against the vernacular. Such a homely and useful word as *piss*, which was good enough for the King James Bible and Dr. Johnson, was cast by Webster into outer dark, along with other "low" words known to everybody but henceforth banned by moral arrogance. Even now, *Merriam-Webster's Third International Unabridged*, wholly revised, pretends that some blunt words don't exist, and as a sole homage to the Founder prints *God* with the only capital letter among all its entries.

For all the types we can fit Webster into—patriot, cultural hero, Calvinist, Federalist, crank—we cannot fit his diversity into any. He was a large man. He moved with energy and ease in his world, discussing spelling reform with Franklin, medicine with Benjamin Rush, and standing on the very steps of Mount Vernon soliciting a blurb from Washington for his spelling book (Washington declined, pleading, with his famous honesty, ignorance of such things). One wishes there were more in this study about Webster the private person, his wife Rebecca, and their children. Rollins makes much of placing Webster in his time, among the turbulent intellectual forces that shaped him and buffeted him, but he neglects to show us Webster at table, in church, in conversation. We are left with an out-of-focus picture of a man who prayed thrice a day and wrote many pamphlets and one stupendous dictionary, but is otherwise invisible. Of his visit, or visits, to Europe we are told nothing. His important work as an educator and as a founder of Amherst might have been traced with more detail.

The effect of this book is to create a lively interest in Webster the man and to follow that interest only in Webster the scholar and polemicist. Perhaps, indeed, he wasn't that kind of figure, so we shall never know him in a pose congenial to the imagination: Jefferson playing his fiddle, Lincoln reading on muleback, John Adams bridling at being read Byron by his daughter, John Marshall dancing in Virginia taverns. I still can see him only as Uriah Heep sniffing out naughty words in the Bible, deleting them, and congratulating himself on being more genteel than God.

The Peales
and Their Museum

Charles Willson Peale (1741–1827), saddle-maker, engraver, portrait painter, soldier in the Revolution, scientist, archaeologist, anthropologist, and inventor of the museum as a democratic school for the people (zoology arranged by phylum, genus, and species; botany; geography; portraits; a menagerie), is one of the few geniuses of whom it can be said that he made a fine art of fatherhood. It was his plan that each of his fourteen children go from the cradle to the easel, the laboratory, or the lecture room. Which, with a slip or two, they did.

They were: Raphaelle, painter; Rembrandt, painter (portraits of Washington, Jefferson, Napoleon); Titian Ramsay the First, a genius who died at eighteen; Titian Ramsay the Second (intended to replace his brother, he became something of a black sheep, fought with Simón Bolívar, explored the West with Maj. Long, and sailed with Wilkes on the famous South Sea and Antarctic expedition); Rubens, who introduced the tomato to Philadelphia and founded the Peale Museum in Baltimore; Angelica, who married Alexander Robinson, a Boston merchant who was ashamed of his in-laws because they painted portraits and hobnobbed with flighty people like Thomas Jefferson and charged the public twenty-five cents a head to see stuffed animals; Sophonisba, who married Coleman Sellers and was the mother of the Escol Sellers who sued Mark Twain when he invented Col. Escol Sellers for *The Gilded Age* (Twain having chosen a name unlikely to have been given an actual human being), and the ancestor of the author of *Mr. Peale's Museum*[1]; Rosalba; Vandyke, who died an infant; Charles Lin-

---

[1] Charles Coleman Sellers, *Mr. Peale's Museum: Charles Willson Peale and the First Popular Museum of Natural Science and Art* (New York: Norton, 1980).

naeus, who named his children Simon Bolivar, Izabella Carapaba, and Hercules Tescier; Aldrovand (a name that was a bit much even for a Peale, after Ulisse Aldrovandi, the sixteenth-century Bolognese naturalist; they got cold feet and renamed him Franklin); and three adopted children: the deaf-mute son of Gen. Hugh Mercer; Charles Peale Polk, a nephew and painter; Betsy, a niece.

He was thrice married. Vandyke, Lin, and Franklin are the children by his second wife. To marry his third, Hannah Moore, Peale had to modify his Deism to conform to her Quaker piety. He outlived them all, and just before he died, in his eighties, he was courting a fourth, to whom he presented as an engagement present a set of Peale's Patented Porcelain Teeth Guaranteed Neither to Yellow nor Decay.

The museum, which lasted from 1784 to its dispersal in 1854, began as a gallery for Peale's portraits. Since the Renaissance there had been collections of curiosities belonging to antiquarians and enthusiasts. None, however, was arranged like a textbook as Peale's was in Philadelphia; none was based on Rousseau's idea of rational entertainment (enjoy and learn); none offered courses of lectures in the evening. Volney, the author of *The Ruins*, an influential and much discussed theory that all tyrannies come to disastrous ends (it caused Shelley to write "Ozymandias"), visted Peale's museum and called it the cathedral of enlightened man. Alexander von Humboldt, the great German naturalist, gave it his admiration, approval, and blessing. Jefferson, a frequent contributor, was one of its most ardent supporters, and if Congress and the Federalists had not been so strongly against it, would have made it our national museum of natural history, a destiny reserved for the Smithsonian, its imitator.

The first triumph of the museum was the mammoth. Bones of this beast had floated around for years, causing all manner of speculation. It was the Great Incognitum. Jefferson, who called it the Ohio Elephant, was a child of his time and believed in the chain of being: the beautifully graduated scheme of creation wherein everything was scaled from low to high—from shrew to whale for the mammals, from minnow to shark for the fish. It was unthinkable that any link in the chain could be missing, and part of Lewis and Clark's orders when they set out was to bring back a mammoth, or Incognitum. (The word *mammoth* Peale got from the zoologist Georges Cuvier, who got it from the Russians; it is the Yakut word *mamont*, meaning "creature-from-the-earth," the *nt* looking in Russian, мамонт, like a typo for *th*, which somebody corrected.)

Peale and a committee of his children traced the source of various mammoth bones which they'd bought to a farm in New York. There (as in the painting Peale made of the scene) they drained a pond with "a mill wheel in reverse," an invention Peale made on the spot, and recovered almost a complete mammoth skeleton. This he articulated, and thus reconstructed the first prehistoric creature. It became the center and mainstay of the museum; the word *mammoth* entered the language, being first used as an adjective by a Philadelphia dairy for its largest cheese. When in 1806 Cuvier decided, with a French sense of things, that its name should be *mastodon* (for its conical teeth, which reminded him of breasts), it was too late to change, and we now use both words. The skeleton itself ended up in P. T. Barnum's travelling show, and was thought to have been lost. It was found after the Second World War in the Museum of Paleontology in Darmstadt, West Germany, where it still stands, though without the skeleton of a mouse at its foot, as Peale always exhibited it.

The museum was an instigator. Alexander Wilson made the first study of American ornithology under its tutelage and inspiration. Audubon derives from it. So did Joseph Henry, of the Smithsonian. It laid groundwork on which Agassiz would build when he came from Switzerland before the Civil War. Practically all our museums, even the technological ones, stem from Peale's seminal idea.

Mr. Peale's Museum is a kind of museum in itself. It has 130 illustrations and a dozen full-color plates of contemporary views, exhibits, and paintings of all the first-generation Peales. The reader who wants to know yet more about this astounding family can turn to Sellers' biography of Charles Willson Peale (1970), the definitive life. The subject is too vast for any one book. You need a whole shelf of biographies and studies to catch the essence of the Peales. Sellers does well within his scope. He gives us a sense of how the museum served as a focus of science in the young Republic, how it cooperated with Franklin's Philosophical Society, how its ambience included the University of Pennsylvania and the Art Institute, how it served and was served by expeditions such as that of Wilkes and Lewis and Clark. It had lines of communication to Paris, Bordeaux, London, and Berlin.

Peale was constantly tempted by the public and by rival imitators to turn his enterprise into a raree-show (as Barnum eventually did when he bought much of the holdings). It was the taste of the public at the time to be pleased more by a two-headed snake than by a normal one; the only concession Peale would make to morbid curiosity was to allow the family cow, who had six legs, to do duty as a *lusus naturae*.

The story of the museum is good solid history, but I suspect that many readers of this book will find themselves fascinated by the harmony and energy of the family. What childhoods! A father was doing successfully what billions in tax dollars and twelve dismal and useless years of schooling fail to do today. Young scientists studied Linnaeus, young taxidermists stuffed Brazilian parrots and Virginia opossums, young artists made whole walls of images. Crates arrived daily from which emerged wildcats, prairie dogs, Carolina marsh hens. One day at breakfast everybody had to scatter before a grizzly bear who had escaped his cage.

Even the servants were artists. The black factotum who sold tickets at the door also did a brisk business in making silhouettes. Raphaelle and Rembrandt, together with their father, left an historical record of their time in portraits and scenes that is one of our greatest cultural heritages. The fine arts and science were integral in their hands; now, in our time, they are not even on speaking terms with each other. A portrait of Rousseau hung over the mantel of their living room, the household god. They could not know that by the Age of Spock and Watson, Rousseau would be perverted beyond all recognition so that personality would replace character; popularity in one's peer group, accomplishment; and easy satisfaction of every whim, the happiness of knowing how to do something well.

It is characteristic of Philadelphia's later indifference to the arts that the city allowed Peale's museum to go under the auctioneer's hammer and be lost forever. No one can see the Revolution and Federalist period as a golden age, no matter how charming it is to imagine the conversation of Jefferson and von Humboldt (try to imagine a conversation between Lévi-Strauss and Reagan), or how astounding it is to consider the skills mastered by a single family, but it was an age that had golden ideals and golden energy.

Pergolesi's Dog

Some dozen years ago, in the middle of one of those conversations which are apt one minute to be about Proust's asthma and the next about the size of chocolate bars in these depraved times, Stan Brakhage, the most advanced guard of filmmakers, asked me if I knew anything about Pergolesi's dog.

Not a thing, I answered confidently, adding that I didn't know he had one. What was there about Pergolesi's dog to know? There, he replied, is the mystery. Just before this conversation, Brakhage had been shooting a film under the direction of Joseph Cornell, the eccentric artist who assembled choice objects in shallow box frames to achieve a hauntingly wonderful, partly surrealistic, partly homemade American kind of art. He lived all his adult life, more or less a recluse, on Utopia Parkway in Flushing, New York, sifting through his boxes of clippings and oddments to find the magic combination of things—a celluloid parrot from Woolworth's, a star map, a clay pipe, a Greek postage stamp—to arrange in a shadow box.

He also made collages and what you could call sculpture, such as dolls in a bed of twigs; and films. For the films he needed a cameraman: thus Brakhage's presence on Utopia Parkway. The two got along beautifully, two geniuses inventing a strange poetry of images (Victorian gingerbread fretwork, fan lights, somber rooms with melancholy windows). Brakhage was fascinated by the shy, erudite Cornell whose hobbies ran to vast dossiers on French ballerinas of the last century, the teachings of Mary Baker Eddy, and the bric-a-brac of all ages and continents.

In one of their talks Pergolesi's dog came up. Brakhage asked what the significance might be of the Italian composer's pet. Cornell bristled. He threw up his hands in profound shock. What! Not know Pergolesi's dog! He had assumed, he said with some frost and disappointment, that he was conversing with a man of culture and sophistication. If Mr. Brakhage could not command an allusion like Pergolesi's dog, would he have the goodness to leave forthwith, and not come back?

Brakhage left. So ended the collaboration of the Republic's most poetic filmmaker and one of its most imaginative artists. The loss is enormous, and it was Pergolesi's dog who caused the rift.

I did the best I could to help Brakhage find this elusive and important dog. He himself had asked everybody in the country who he thought might know. I asked. The people we asked, they in turn asked others. Biographies and histories were of no help. No one knew anything about a dog belonging to, or in the society of, Giovanni Battista Pergolesi. For ten years I asked likely people, and when my path crossed Brakhage's I would shake my head, and he would shake his: no d. of P. yet found.

We never considered that Cornell was as ignorant of Pergolesi's dog as we. In Samuel Butler II's *Notebooks* there is this instructive entry: "Zeffirino Carestia, a sculptor, told me we had a great sculptor in England named Simpson. I demurred, and asked about his work. It seemed he had made a monument to Nelson in Westminster Abbey. Of course I saw he meant Stevens, who made a monument to Wellington in St. Paul's. I cross-questioned him and found I was right."

We are never so certain of our knowledge as when we're dead wrong. The assurance with which Chaucer included Alcibiades in a list of beautiful women and with which Keats embedded the wrong discoverer of the Pacific in an immortal sonnet should be a lesson to us all.

Ignorance achieves wonders. The current *Encyclopaedia Britannica* informs us that Edmund Wilson's *Axel's Castle* is a novel (it is a book of essays), that Eudora Welty wrote *Clock without Hands* (by Carson McCullers), and that the photograph of Jules Verne accompanying the entry about him is of a Yellow-Headed Titmouse (*Auriparus flaviceps*). The *New York Review of Books* once referred to *The Petrarch Papers* of Dickens and a nodding proofreader for the *TLS* once let Margery Allingham create a detective named Albert Camus.

Vagueness has vernacular charm. A footnote in a Shaker hymnal identifies George Washington as "one of our first presidents."

Cornell when he had his tizzy about Pergolesi's dog was beyond vagueness and into the certainty of the dead wrong. Sooner or later I was bound to luck onto the right person, who, as it turned out, was wise to Cornell's waywardness with bits of trivia. This was John Bernard Myers, art critic and dealer. What Cornell meant, he felt sure, was Borgese's dog. I looked as blank as Brakhage had on the previous, fatal occasion. What! Not know Borgese's dog!

Elisabeth Mann Borgese, daughter of Thomas, professor of political science at Dalhousie University, the distinguished ecologist and conservationist, had trained a dog in the 1940s to type answers to questions on a special machine that fitted its paws. The success of this undertaking is still dubious in scientific circles, but the spectacle it made at the keyboard of its machine stuck in Joseph Cornell's mind as one of the events of the century, and he supposed that all well-informed people were familiar with it. La Borgese's accomplished beast's habit of typing BAD DOG when it had flubbed a right answer had brought tears to his eyes. He had a dossier of clippings about all this, and despite its sea-change in his transforming imagination, had no qualms about dismissing people tediously ignorant of such wonderful things.

Late Beckett

Study a rotation of the second hand on your wristwatch. It has a shadow which it eclipses every thirtieth second. For half of its round the shadow follows the second hand, for the other half it precedes it. The shadow is at its maximum distance from the second hand mid-arc the two occlusions. The symmetries of this cunning hairline of a shadow can beguile your attention for as long as you want to study them. You have, for instance, an accelerated hothouse sundial that nips along 1,440 times faster than the real article; you have a simple model of the solar system; you have something to keep you company.

Almost at the end of Samuel Beckett's new prose narrative we are told that if "numb with the woes of your kind you raise none the less your head from off your hands and open your eyes" you can study the second hand of your watch and "hours later" have the relationship of it to its shadow worked out. This is the only action in the narrative, the only flex of plot.

Much else, nevertheless, is there in the text, suspended in uncertainty, approached with agonized hesitation. We know by now that any fact in a Beckett novel can be snatched away. Here, in *Company*,[1] we are not even allowed the luxury of the author committing himself to a character, much less to a plot or setting.

We are instead invited to suppose (and identify with) a being lying on its back in total dark to whom an unidentifiable voice says, "You are on your back in the dark." The being cannot reply, having no power to speak. Nor can it know that the voice is speaking to it (and not, for instance, to some

[1]Samuel Beckett, *Company* (New York: Grove Press, 1980).

other being on its back in the same dark). The being has only this voice "for company."

Is the being on its back in the dark company for the disembodied voice? Such an unanswerable question generates other unanswerable questions. And then there is the suspicion that the voice is not from outside but from within: memory itself. For sporadically it (or plausibly the being, summoning memories and addressing itself as "you") recounts events from a childhood. These brief scenes are like magic-lantern slides which appear on the wall without program or intelligible sequence, and leave the dark darker when they go away with the same arbitrariness as they came.

One of these Proustian glows from the past cannot be the memory of the being on its back, for it describes its father's anguish on the day of its birth, a remote day when a De Dion Bouton was a make of automobile. Moreover, it was a Good Friday. The father and the birthdate correspond with those of Beckett, as do other events which we can find in Deirdre Bair's biography[2]—such as the child Beckett launching himself from the top of a fir tree to see if he could fly.

So the being on its back, first introduced as a tentative character, as if to see what could be worked out in the way of a narrative, becomes the writer himself. This identification, however, is repeatedly rejected with the phrase, "Quick leave him." (The only punctuation in this book is the period. Beckett gave up the semicolon years ago, and the comma several books back.)

Beckett's art has over the years dared itself to do without various necessities. Here, for instance, he begins a game in which he denies himself the first-person-singular pronoun. This is a feint, for by page eight there it is, triumphantly necessary after all ("Yes I remember"). What this feint was hiding was the suppression not of "I" but the companionable "we."

A writer is a deviser. "Devised deviser devising it all for company," muses the text. Is the text by Beckett; that is, by an author telling us a narrative? Is the text devised, as, say, the text of *Waiting for Godot*, for an actor to speak? This problem is the plot of *Company*. It is the old problem of the dominance of the subjective or the objective in a work of art. The problem is footling: are we to meditate on the humanistic expressiveness of Michelangelo in gazing at the *David*, or are we to forget Michelangelo and pay full attention to the image of heroism, beauty, and piety which the artist worked so hard to show us?

In a sense *Company* is Beckett's reply to Deirdre Bair's biography, a book which could only have been embarrassing to him, and which seemed to

[2]Deirdre Bair, *Samuel Beckett: A Biography* (New York: Harcourt Brace Jovanovich, 1978).

many reviewers to be an outrageous invasion of his privacy. Yet he cooperated, in a way, with its writing. He agreed neither to help Bair nor to stand in
her way. *Company* is a meditation on the creator and the created. The privacy which a biographer seems to violate is inviolable. And whereas the
biographer can only operate with *reportage* and surmise, the artist works on
the same material with the one thing the biographer must eschew: the imagination.

Beckett's imagination has always been distinguished by what we might
call comic alertness. Committed to his discipline of compression, exactitude
of word and phrase, of paring everything to the bone, he uses this absolute
carefulness of composition as a breeding ground for the comic. No joke,
however wry, is allowed to get away; no irony, however sardonic, is excluded.

Company replays Beckett's central problem in all his work. Man, whatever he is (cosmic joke? puppet of a divine puppeteer? mistake of a frivolous
and cruel God? a creature a little less than the angels in majesty who has
disobediently, stubbornly, and stupidly alienated himself from every blessing?), has no way of being certain about anything. The masterful plays *Waiting for Godot* and *Endgame* were written around the maddeningly teasing
uncertainty of the Christian *mythos*. Mr. Godot sends to say that he won't
be coming today but will most certainly get here tomorrow. What a nerve-
wracking religion: it promises an arrival. Its adherents have been waiting
for 1,955 years for a return promised "soon." Or is it 1,950 years, as the
counters of time idiotically have Christ born on His fifth birthday? Has He
already returned, say in 922 or 1934, and we stupidly missed the fact as millions did when He first came?

Endgame is a crucifixion in slow motion—not all of it, only the moment
when Christ cried out in despair. The being on its back in the dark in *Company* considers every possibility of knowing its identity and condition except
that of being held against the wall of a centrifuge, with the spin of time
speeded up to hold him there (like, for instance, the speed of that second hand
compared with the slower tick of time as we are damned to perceive it). And
not a wall, but a cross. "What kind of imagination is this so reason-hidden?"
somebody asks in *Company*. And somebody answers, "A kind of its own."

No character in Beckett has ever admitted that existence is other than a
cruel joke. But here in *Company* Beckett reaches into a darker dark than he
has hitherto plumbed, to ask if the poor jokester didn't, after all, create us,
his joke, to keep his lonely self company? This is a way of asking if in our
profound and agonizing loneliness we have invented the jokester, God, to

keep ourselves company? And what is company? What have we not done
for its sake? For everything human we have made up, beginning with our
names. Our laws, our quaint systems of kinship, our cities, our technology,
a Victorian clergyman's carefully researched study of the Sumerian cosmol-
ogy—fiction all. We've made it all up, to hide a mystery in an idiotically dec-
orated box. The only reality is that we became aware of the world on our
back in the dark (the womb, the cradle), with a voice speaking to us, and will
end on our backs in the dark (deathbed, grave). Beckett in *Company* con-
nects these two points of existential helplessness. We are forever on our
backs in the dark, listening to a voice (dreams, the imagination, philosophy,
religion, Walter Cronkite). But, as he says, the voice is company, or we are
company for it.

Every Force
Evolves a Form

Jesus said: Split a stick. I will be inside.
THE GOSPEL OF THOMAS [77]

Split the Lark, and you'll find the Music,
Bulb after Bulb, in Silver rolled.
EMILY DICKINSON

1835

A robin entered a Westmorland cottage in which a child lay ill with a fever and an old woman, senile, sat by the fire. The robin was greeted as a *daimon*, an elemental spirit, whose presence was understood to be a good omen. Of this event Wordsworth, who was sixty-four, made a poem, "The Redbreast."

1845

A raven entered the room of a man in grief and drove him to madness by replying "Nevermore" to all questions put to it, as the man, aware that the bird was in effect an automaton, a bird capable of vocal mimicry but with a vocabulary of one word only, persisted in treating the raven as if it were supernatural and capable of answering questions about the fate of the soul after death.

1855

An osprey, swooping and crying with a "barbaric yawp" (both words referring to sound, speech that is not Greek and seems to be *bar bar* over and over, *yawp*, a word as old as English poetry itself for the strident or hoarse call of a bird) seemed to Walt Whitman to be a *daimon* upbraiding him for his "gab and loitering." Whitman replied (at the end of the first section of *Leaves of Grass*, in later editions the fifty-second and closing part of "Song of Myself") that he was indeed very like the osprey, "not a bit tamed," sounding *his* "barbaric yawp over the roofs of the world." And like the hawk he speaks with the authority of nature. We must make of his message what we will. "If you want me again look for me under your boot-soles."

> You will hardly know who I am or what I mean,
> But I shall be good health to you nevertheless,
> And filter and fibre your blood.

> Failing to fetch me at first keep encouraged,
> Missing me one place search another,
> I stop somewhere waiting for you.

Thereafter in *Leaves of Grass* birds are understood to be *daimons*. Poe's man in grief was sure that the raven was a prophet, but whether "bird or devil" ("Whether Tempter sent, or whether tempest tossed thee here ashore") he did not know. Whitman was remembering this line when in "Out of the Cradle Endlessly Rocking" he asked if the mocking-bird, the *daimon* of that poem, be "Demon or bird."

1877

In the fields around St. Beuno's College in North Wales a thirty-three-year-old Jesuit named Gerard Manley Hopkins observed a kestrel, or windhover, riding the air. Remembering the hawk that fixed a lyric vision in Walt Whitman's heart (Whitman's mind, he wrote later, was "like my own"), he took the moment to be a revelation of Whitman's spirit "somewhere waiting for you." That his prophetic words would stir the heart of an English poet to see Christ as a raptor of souls would have pleased Whitman. We can also assume that he would have admired the younger poet's obvious rivalry in the art of fitting words to images and rhythms to emotions. *Minion* is Whitmanesque. "Dapple dawn-drawn Falcon, in his riding / Of the rolling level underneath him steady air, and striding / High there" bests Whitman's "The spotted hawk swoops by," the "last scud of day hold[ing] back" for it. Whitman's osprey is seen with the last of the day's sun on it, its height enabling it to be still sunlit while Whitman at ground level is in the "shadow'd wilds" of dusk. Hopkin's windhover is seen catching the first of the sun before dawn has reached the Welsh fields beneath it.

ROBIN

The robin in Wordsworth is a herald of inspiration after a fallow time, of recovery from an illness, and of heaven itself. In Book VII of *The Prelude*, a renewal of poetic power is announced by

> A choir of red-breasts gathered somewhere near
> My threshold, — minstrels from the distant woods
> Sent in on Winter's service, to announce,
> With preparation artful and benign,
> That the rough lord had left the surly North. . . .

The robin in "The Redbreast" has similarly come into the cottage by the on-coming of winter.

> Driven in by Autumn's sharpening air
> From half-stripped woods and pastures bare,
> Brisk Robin seeks a kindlier home. . . .

Note Robin: a proper name. Birds assigned names, as well as animals, constitute a series which Lévi-Strauss discusses in *The Savage Mind*, in a chapter titled "The Individual as Species." In French the fox is Reynard, the swan Godard, the sparrow Pierrot, and so on. *Erithacus rubecula* is already Robin Redbreast in Middle English, by which time it was established throughout Europe as one of the Little Birds of Christ's Passion (with much folklore about how its breast was reddened by Christ's blood, hell fire, and the like). It is obvious that Wordsworth hears its name as if it were analogous to Harold Bluetooth, rather than to Jack Daw, Jim Crow, or John Dory. Hence its ruddy breast is "a natural shield / Charged with a blazon on the field." This alignment with chivalric insignia is important, as Wordsworth is articulating a tradition whereby the robin can be thoroughly of the matter of Britain: it has an elf in it (Chaucer, Jonson); it is a kind of Red Cross Knight; it is equally Christian and pagan (Spenser), while being principally the bird *daimon* that we can trace to European prehistory, and which became the chief symbol of poetic inspiration for the Romantics (Shelley, Keats, Tennyson, Poe, Whitman).

PARROT OWL RAVEN

Poe's imagery resolves into three styles, each constituting a dialect with its own grammar and poetic purpose. His own names for these styles were the Arabesque, the Grotesque, and the Classic. In the early stages of planning "The Raven" he considered a parrot and an owl. A parrot would have required that the poem's dominant style be Arabesque; an owl, Classic. As it is, he managed to have the parrot's echoic mimicry implicit in the repetition of *nevermore* (which is not an echo, unless the bird is trying to say "Night's Plutonian shore"); and the owl was translated into its divine equivalent, the bust of Pallas on which the raven perches.

ONE CALVINIST CROW

Poe's raven is an automaton, a machine programmed to say a single word. If a man, half mad with grief, takes it for an oracle and asks it questions, he can see his error or he can persist in projecting onto the raven his desperate hope that he has the use of an oracle. Thus the raven, asked its name, answers, "Nevermore." The grief-stricken man observes bitterly and hysterically that not even his loneliness will be alleviated by the bird named Nevermore, for it too, like his friends and hopes, will abandon him "on the morrow." To this the raven replies, "Nevermore." It is here that the man realizes that the raven's vocabulary consists of one word. Madness, however, has its own logic. The bird, for instance, may have been sent by God to help him forget his grief, and if sent by God, may therefore have theological wisdom. So he asks it if there is balm in Gilead. Meaning? "Will I be comforted in my loss by faith? Will I be united with Lenore in Heaven? Is there a Heaven? Is there life after death? Is Lenore with God? Does God exist?" The question is Jeremiah's, at 8:22, "Is there no balm in Gilead?" Jeremiah was asking, by way of rhetorical flourish, if Newcastle has no coal. Poe transformed the meaning to: is there really a Newcastle, and is there coal there? To which Nevermore replies, "Nevermore." The next question is blunter: will he ever be reunited with Lenore? "Nevermore." The speaker orders the raven out of his house, and the raven refuses ever to leave. And never is also when the speaker's soul will be disentangled from the raven's shadow; his despair is permanent.

Poe had met the situation before. In Richmond he had seen Maelzel's machine that played chess, and saw through it (guessing, rightly, that it had a man concealed in it). In both the chess-playing machine and the univerbal raven Poe was looking at Presbyterian theology: all is predestined, or some human intermediary wants us to believe that it is. Worse, we are disposed by our helplessness in grief, despair, or bewilderment to cooperate with the idea of mechanized fate. After reason has acted, we can still find a residue of superstition. There is a part of our reason willing to believe that automata have minds. In that dark space Poe wrote. The ape in "The Murders in the Rue Morgue" is an automaton, as Roderick Usher is a zombie when he buries his sister alive. Calvin and Newton both gave us a machine for a world, a gearwork of inevitabilities.

DARWINIAN MOCKING-BIRD

Whitman's reply to "The Raven" is "Out of the Cradle Endlessly Rocking."
Again, an oracle is questioned. The answer (from bird and the sound of the sea
together) is polyphonic, *love* and *death* together. Life and death are a Hera-
clitean rhythm, independent. Whitman returns to the Greek sense that love is
deepest in its tragic awareness of the brevity of life, of youth, of beauty.

TIME

Time for Poe was the monotonous tick of the universe, the unstoppable tread
of death, coming closer second by second (like walls closing in, the swing of a
pendulum, the sealing up of a wall brick by brick, footsteps evenly mounting
a stair). Whitman's time was tidal, migratory, the arousal and satisfaction of
desire. Hopkins knew that time was over at the moment it began, that it has
no dimensions, that Christ on the cross cancelled all adverbs. There is no
soon, no *never*. There is only the swoop of the hawk, the eyes that say *follow
me* to the fisherman, the giddy ecstasy of *I stop somewhere waiting for you*.

11 MAY 1888: WHITMAN IN CAMDEN, TALKING

"Do I like Poe? At the start, for many years, not: but three or four years ago
I got to reading him again, reading and liking, until at last—yes, now—I feel
almost convinced that he is a star of considerable magnitude, if not a sun, in
the literary firmament. Poe was morbid, shadowy, lugubrious—he seemed
to suggest dark nights, horrors, spectralities—I could not originally stomach him at all. But today I see more of him than that—much more. If that
was all there was to him he would have died long ago. I was a young man of
about thirty, living in New York, when The Raven appeared—created its
stir: everybody was excited about it—every reading body: somehow it did
not enthuse me." [Whitman had given "Out of the Cradle Endlessly Rocking" its final revision (it was written in 1859) the year before, and placed it at
the heart of the new "Sea-Drift" section of the 1881 *Leaves of Grass*.]

QUICK, SAID THE BIRD, FIND THEM, FIND THEM

The history of birds taken to be *daimons* traverses religions, folklore, and
literature. In Europe it begins with the drawing of a bird mounted on a pole
in Lascaux. In the New World we can trace it back to the Amerindian understanding of the meadowlark as a mediator between men and spirits of the air.
Poe's raven, Keats' nightingale, Shelley's skylark, Olson's kingfisher, Whitman's osprey, thrush, and mocking-bird, Hopkins' windhover are but mod-
ulations in a long tradition, a dance of forms to a perennial spiritual force.

Making It Uglier
to the Airport

Every building in the United States is an offense to invested capital. It occupies space which, as greed acknowledges no limits, can be better utilized. This depressing fact can be thought of as a kind of disease of the American city for which the only specific is law, and, to make a wild gesture toward common sense, aesthetics. One might as well say that multiple sclerosis can be cured with cough drops.

In Chicago six years ago they tore down Adler and Sullivan's Old Stock Exchange, a perfectly useful building. That it was bone and blood of Chicago history, that it was an architectural landmark, that its ornamentation was beautiful and irreplaceable were arguments that could not save it. Money has no ears, no eyes, no respect; it is all gut, mouth, and ass. The Heller International Building went up in its place, a glass cracker-box forty-three stories high. Its mortgage payments are $400,000 every first of the month: interest—*interest*, money which bankers earn by tightening their shoelaces, yawning, and testing teakwood surfaces for dust—on a $48,300,000 loan. The building cost $51,000,000, and is up for grabs, as the speculators can't hold onto it. This time nobody cares if, as they shall, they tear it down and put up something more "economically viable," as they say.

Heaps of New York are being torn down because what's left over after property taxes isn't quite what our greedy hearts would like to take to our investment broker. Between the banker and the tax-collector, life can be very hell. But then, they built the cities in the first place. One of the greatest of architects built snowmen for the Medici children (a use of Michelangelo we would have expected of J. Pierpont Morgan sooner than Lorenzo the Magnificent); all architects are now sculptors in ice.

Ada Louise Huxtable, who writes about architecture and city planning for the *Times*, has collected a batch of her terse essays on buildings going up and coming down, on design, and practically anything else that her lively eye hits on.[1] Her comments are all arrows of the chase, released when the aim seemed good, and with some fine hits. Like all such writing, you can feel the pressure of the deadline on her attention. She turns up many problems (the war, apparently to the death, between city design and real-estate adventurers; the coherence of American cityscape; the preservation of landmarks; the tension between contemporaneity and tradition) that I would like to have seen her expand and explore.

While I was reading her essays, I happened to run across Manfredo Tafuri's *Architecture and Utopia: Design and Capitalist Development*, which I saw in the MIT catalogue when I was ordering Dolores Hayden's fine survey of American utopian communities.[2] Tafuri traces the decay and disorder of cities to the rise of commercial centers during the industrial revolution, causing cities to enter a paranoia of identity. His little book is worth reading—worth studying with care—but it gleams and blinds with too much Marxist intellect for me to pretend to discuss it here. The one idea that I want to take from it is that what we call a city bears little resemblance to the historical city or to cities outside the United States. Yet our cities still sit on top of a living archaeological base that used to be a city in the old sense. The automobile and the truck have shaved the yards to mere margins in the quiet residential sections; the streets have become freeways all over every city and town. Automobile exhaust, equal in volume daily to that of the Atlantic Ocean, has replaced breathable air. The automobile is an insect that eats cities, and its parking lots are a gangrene.

The simple fact is that cities in America came into being not as the historical city did, for mutual protection and to be the home of a specific family of people, but as commercial ports. That is, their model was the kind of prosperous city Defoe describes in the first inventory the mercantile class made of itself, his *Tour Thro' the Whole Island of Great Britain* (1724–26). All important elements were in walking distance of each other; *nearness* defined the city. If it grew large, each neighborhood (as in Paris and London today) remained a conglomerate of components within easy reach.

[1]Ada Louise Huxtable, *Kicked a Building Lately?* (New York: Quadrangle, 1976).
[2]Manfredo Tafuri, *Architecture and Utopia: Design and Capitalist Development*, trans. Barbara Luigia La Penta (Cambridge: MIT Press, 1976). Dolores Hayden, *Seven American Utopias: The Architecture of Communitarian Socialism, 1790–1975* (Cambridge: MIT Press, 1976).

Within the last twenty years the automobile has gradually cancelled this definition of the city as a community. And the smaller the city, the larger the inconvenience has grown. When I moved to Lexington, Kentucky, fifteen years ago, I could walk to three supermarkets in my neighborhood, to the post office, and to the mayor's house, which happened to be around the corner. All three markets have moved miles away, to the belt line; God knows where they have put the post office. I have been there but once since they moved it. It took me an hour to get there, and an hour to get back. It is technically in the next county, and is near no habitation of any citizen. Only some desolate warehouses does it have for company. This happened when Nixon and his government of scoundrels, liars, and sneaks had us *scrotum in mano* and I assumed that sheer hatefulness snatched the post office from downtown and put it out in the horse pastures.

The post office, in any case, was only good for buying stamps at. When I tried to renew my passport there a few years ago, a passport kept functional for thirty years, I was told that if I couldn't show a driver's license I couldn't renew my passport. (I will not spin out the Gogolian scene that ensued, though it featured my being told that I didn't deserve to live in this country, my pointing out that I could scarcely leave it without a passport, and on around in circles that left the art of Gogol for that of Ionesco, until I got the State Department on the phone, and had my new passport, together with an apology, in three days.) The point of the anecdote is that the pedestrian is officially a second-rate citizen and definitely an obsolete species.

Where the mayor moved to I do not know. The neighborhood is now zoned for business. Henry Clay's townhouse, part of the neighborhood, sits in a tarred-over parking lot.[3]

I had not realized before reading Dolores Hayden's *Seven American Utopias* that the Civil War marked the end of utopian experimentation in American communities. We now know how very much of modern design derives from Shaker clarity and integrity, and how useful, if only as models to modify or tolerate, the Owenite, Fourierist, Moravian, and other eccentric societies were.

Acceleration in culture is demonic, and there ought to be periodic recesses to look back and reclaim elements that were ditched along the way. To read Dolores Hayden is to see how much we elbowed aside, or smothered, or de-

[3]There is an excellent essay on the kinds of cities bequeathed us by history as paradigms, in *Salmagundi* No. 24 (Fall 1973), "The City under Attack" by George Steiner. This is a rich essay, with long historical perspectives. He shows us that much of what we take to be peculiarly modern ills are in fact very old, and that our double tradition, classical and Judaeo-Christian, gives us two distinct ideas of what a city is.

liberately obliterated. Fourier's phalanx seems to be a congenial mode of life that might have forestalled our present alienation of the young, the old, and the lonely. Shaker respect for materials is certainly the corrective we need for our present norm of tacky shoddiness, for mushroom proliferation. Shaker morals wouldn't be amiss, either.

Backward surveys can also turn up some astonishing forks in the road. Alison Sky and Michelle Stone have compiled what amounts to a treasury of American designs, from cities to individual buildings, that never made it from the blueprint into actuality.[4] One purpose of this book was to assess our architectural legacy—designs, for instance, that might still be realized. There is a postmortem career awaiting Frank Lloyd Wright; all great architects are ahead of their times. Sadly, many of these plans have been chucked into the wastebasket. An architect's firm is a business, not an archive. Not even so distinguished a figure as Frederick Law Olmsted was spared this kind of careless destruction. A vigorous society might well build Thomas Jefferson's President's House, if only in Disneyland, where, in effect, Jacques J. B. Benedict's Summer Capitol for President Woodrow Wilson (projected for Mt. Falcon, Colorado) already stands—it looks like an Arthur Rackham drawing for Mad Ludwig of Bavaria. Many of these rejected designs are lugubrious and hilarious: a robber-baron New Versailles for Manhasset Bay, Long Island, that would have been the biggest building in the world, something that Hitler and Albert Speer might have drooled over; art-book cathedrals recapitulating the whole span of the Gothic in Europe, beacons taller than Everest, Babylonian banks, war memorials that would have trivialized the Pyramids, linear towns with highways for halls, space islands, underground metropolises, a New Harmony phalanx that looks like a Victorian penitentiary crossbred with Flash Gordon's spacecraft port. And yet these designs are full of attractive and charming ideas: a Manhattan with separate thoroughfares for pedestrians and traffic, garden cities, beautiful vistas that would have made Chicago as handsome as Paris, and buildings that ought to have existed for the fun of it, William McKinley Xanadus, palaces, follies—outrageous flowers for the granite forest.

The depressing obliteration of communities can sometimes be as thorough as Noah's Flood. New Burlington, Ohio, a town between Dayton and Cincinnati, is now at the bottom of a lake created, as it often seems, to keep the Army Corps of Engineers busy. Before New Burlington went under, an extraordinarily sensitive writer, John Baskin, talked with the old-timers and

[4]Alison Sky and Michelle Stone, *Unbuilt America: Forgotten Architecture in the United States from Thomas Jefferson to the Space Age* (New York: McGraw-Hill, 1976).

recorded their memories. The resulting book is poignant and, if you're in a reflective mood or of a pessimistic turn, heartbreaking. The obituary of an entire town has the aura of doom all over it. The only horror of death is in waiting for it, and here was a community that knew its doom: not of life, but of so much of it that the difference perhaps is not accountable. The terror of Hektor's death was that, moments before his heart tasted Achilles' blade, he had to run past places where he had played as a boy. John Baskin carefully avoids dramatics in this book. His business was to hear the past. In the process, however, it dawned on him that American life has changed. What's different is that whereas just a few years ago we all had something to do, now we don't.

It is tempting to believe that New Burlington, Ohio, was built before the Civil War (partly by Methodists, partly by Quakers) by people for whom skill and hard work were as natural a fact as breathing, and that it went underwater because a society had emerged that is neurotic with idleness and pointlessness. (The Red River Gorge in Kentucky was saved from flooding by the Corps of Engineers because when our governor asked the corps *why* they wanted to obliterate so much natural beauty, they could not give an answer.)

It is good to know, on the other hand, that a small community can fight and can win against the restless greed of investment capital and botchers of all breeds. A nameless town in California has so far held out over a sudden influx of developers and do-gooders working together. The do-gooders noticed the town when it was gunked up by an oil spill (halt and give some time to the ironies that crisscross here). During the cleanup it was noticed that the community had an inadequate sewer system. This attracted the money boys from a water company, who convinced the state that vast sums must be spent to get everybody onto a flushing toilet. This alerted the osmagogue bankers, who alerted the real-estate gang. As long as this community—half retired folk, largely hermits, half young utopians who had fled the city—was to be modernized, so thought the developers, let's pop in resort hotels, Burger Kings, miniature golf, redwood-shingle condominiums, and let's see these old geezers and hippies clear the hell out.

The struggle and triumph of this commuity (not named, for its own protection) is presented in a thoroughly good book.[5] Orville Schell, who has written well and humanely about Chinese communes, shows how a community that is eccentric, almost centerless, and even casual, can knit together

[5] Orville Schell, *The Town That Fought to Save Itself*, with photographs by Ilka Hartmann (New York: Pantheon Books, 1976).

and drive away the bulldozer, sanitary engineer, and real-estate shark. He presents his problem in a paragraph that it would be brutal to paraphrase:

> A town which is a community is a delicate organism. As yet, it has virtually no legal means at its disposal by which to protect itself from those who choose to search it out. Unlike an individual, it cannot sue for invasion of privacy. It cannot effectively determine how many people can live in it. It cannot even decide for itself the number of visitors with which it feels comfortable. The roads are there; anyone may travel on them. A commercial establishment is free to advertise the town's name and its desirable attributes in the hopes of attracting people to it in order to make money. If the people who call that town home find the influx of people, cars, and money unsettling, they have little recourse.

If those words were attributed to a New England Conservative complaining about Italian immigrants, or to Robert Moses complaining about the influx of Puerto Ricans, they would outrage Liberal ears. Paradoxically they illustrate how accurately we must understand a writer's point of view. "Organism" is the word to hold onto. Schell's words are true, and astutely stated. The nature of the organism determines what kind of turbulence it can tolerate.

Poland survived the Second World War better than my hometown in South Carolina. Main Street has rotted into a wasteland. Gracious old homes came down to make way for used-car lots, tacky little finance companies, and drive-in hamburger pavilions. The seven ancient oaks that stood around the house where Thomas Wolfe's sister lived fell to the power saw, and the house itself, deporched, hoked up with neon and Coca-Cola signs, was islanded in a desolation of tar paving and converted into an eatery called, with that genius of the destroyer for taunting, The Seven Oaks. Some two miles of magnolia shade became a glare of festooned light bulbs, and all the used-car dealers are named Shug and Bubber, a semiology I am not equipped to explore. The ugliness of it all is visual migraine. And yet a mayor and his councilmen let it happen. The American politician may be a psychological type, like the kleptomaniac, peeping tom, or exhibitionist. He is the only professional who may apply for a job and present as his credentials the blatant and unashamed fact that he has none. (Lincoln Steffens was surprised to discover that city management throughout Europe requires a college degree.) But the explanation of why our cities are being uglified is not to be found wholly in political venality, capitalistic exploitation, greed, carelessness, or any one force.

The history of a city ought to disclose how it came to be what it is. John and LaRee Caughey have put together a composite "history" of that monster metropolis Los Angeles.[6] The apologies for the word *history* are because the book is an anthology of short passages from over a hundred writers. The method seems appropriate for a sprawling subject, the locale of such contrasts (Hollywood and Watts, UCLA and Sunset Boulevard). I suspect the book is of greatest interest to Angelenos themselves, though it is a marvellous book to read around in. It makes the tacit assumption that no American city of such size can be got between the pages of a book. The word *history* is wonderfully tricky when applied to a city. One can write the history of England better than the history of London. In another sense, the history of Los Angeles can be written sometime in the next century, but not now.

A more thorough and integral history of a city is of Roger Sale's of Seattle.[7] This is a model of how city histories should be written. Seattle is a perfect example of the American city in that it was not an accidental pooling of settlers in its beginning, but a deliberate act by stalwart citizens who had come to found a city. The university, the neighborhoods, the businesses, the bank, practically all the elements were decided on as the first buildings went up. We think of the westward expansion as so many pioneers clearing the wilderness for *farms*; that's mythology—they were colonists who had the plans of cities in their heads, the first since Greeks and Romans set out from *mother cities* (*metropolites*) to reproduce examples of the model they came from.

Prof. Sale, a highly skilled and spirited writer, gives us each epoch of Seattle's history in fine detail. He knows that cities are really so many people, and inserts full biographies throughout. He gives a lucid account of the city's economic and sociological history; he knows its institutions and newspapers. Most importantly, he knows the city's lapses and false steps; not a syllable of chauvinism or whitewashing mars these pages. The book is therefore vigorous in its honesty and in the range of its considerations; it is as good on labor leaders (Dave Beck) as on intellectuals (Vernon Parrington). It is a speculative book that can discuss the benefit of good high schools and parks, and can explain how the American labor movement, which by rights ought to have emerged as leftist and radical (as the Seattle friend of Mao, Anna Louise Strong, urged), became rightist and conservative.

A city's history can be done in finer and finer detail. You can zone off a decade, as Michael Lesy has done with the twenties in Louisville, or study

[6]John and LaRee Caughey, *Los Angeles: Biography of a City* (Berkeley: University of California Press, 1976).
[7]Roger Sale, *Seattle, Past to Present* (Seattle: University of Washington Press, 1976).

neighborhoods family by family, as Roslyn Banish has done with a London and a Chicago neighborhood, or trace a single family through six generations.[8] Lesy, who began his method of composite history with *Wisconsin Death Trip*, repeats that work with Louisville in Prohibition times. Using photographs from the commercial firm of Caulfield and Shook, police and insane-asylum records, he constructs, with what seems to me like morbidity and gratuitous cynicism, a sustained surrealistic picture of the period. His point, of course, is that's the way they chose to see themselves—Masons in all their gaudy trappings, blacks at lodge banquets, society folk looking superior, T-Model wrecks, prehistoric Gulf stations, promotion photos by go-getter salesmen. A lot of the surrealism is, I'm afraid, mere psychological tone. Similar photographs of the 1860s we would perceive as History. These things come in phases: today's junk is tomorrow's antique, etc., but the process has some subtle quality one can't pin down. Lesy makes the age seem indecent; I grew up in it, and don't remember it that way at all. The present moment is far tackier (he would probably agree), and it is true, as he claims, that newspapers speak in a tongue all their own. And all documents in a neutral voice (police recorder, case histories from the asylum) tell us more about the institution keeping such files than about the subject. It is Lesy's hope that raw documents speak for themselves, and that captionless photographs are powerfully meaningful. I have my doubts. The method seems to me to be a bit cocky and fraudulent. The truth of a period cannot be summoned by a few eloquent photographs and a batch of newspaper clippings. It is the equivalent of trying to understand the Second World War from newsreels alone.

Roslyn Banish supplements her photographs of London and Chicago families with responsible statistics and with commentaries by the subjects themselves. She also allowed the subjects to choose their setting (almost invariably the best-looking room, as they thought) and pose. Ms. Banish is a canny photographer, giving us in splendid light just enough detail to complete the portraits (a coat hanger inexplicably in a living room, a dimestore Gainsborough over a policeman's mantel), and an even cannier sociologist to have conceived and carried out her project. She has made a book from which one learns about people in a particular and piquant way without any violation of their privacy, without condescension, and with gentleness to-

[8]Michael Lesy, *Real Life: Louisville in the Twenties* (New York: Pantheon Books, 1976). Roslyn Banish, *City Families: Chicago and London* (New York: Pantheon Books, 1976). Dorothy Gallagher, *Hannah's Daughters: Six Generations of an American Family: 1876–1976* (New York: Crowell, 1976).

ward their vulnerability. There is more respect for human beings in these photographs than I have ever seen a photographer achieve. One falls in love with the eighty-year-old Alice Williams in the first photograph (lovebirds, electric heater, paper flowers) and remains in awe of the dignity of these homefolks right up to a smiling Irish Chicago police sergeant in the last. I liked Douglas Humphreys (butler, Buckingham Palace), who looks like the Hon. Gally Threepwood in Wodehouse, part of whose interview recalls a buffet supper for heads of state after Churchill's funeral: "I was entertaining myself a few moments with Mr. Khrushchev. Oh yes, now he had two bodyguards and an interpreter with him. I took off his greatcoat and I felt the eyes of those burly guards. I hung his greatcoat up and I said to the interpreter, 'Just tell your two men to relax. I'm on duty on the occasion of Her Majesty's Royal Household.' And I added, 'One day I should like to pay a visit to your country, sir.' He . . . actually shook hands." One feels that Humphreys was *comforting* Comrade K., and not even Trollope could have thought of such a wonderful moment.

Dorothy Gallagher's *Hannah's Daughters* is an oral history, taken down in a series of interviews, of six generations of a Washington family of Dutch descent, members of all of them being alive in August 1973, a chain of daughters reaching from the ninety-seven-year-old Hannah to her two-year-old great-great-great-granddaughter. The hundred photographs illustrating the narratives progress from tintype to Polaroid. The text has the interest of good talk, and covers a great deal of American history in very American voices: ". . . everybody was kissing everybody. It was really something. That was V-E Day. It was absolutely wild. I didn't think there *were* that many people." Gertrude Stein would have liked this book, and even tried to write it, the wrong way round, in *The Making of Americans*. Family history has traditionally been a woman's preserve. And what a distance there is from "They'd kill a hog and I'd get the fat cleaned off the hog intestines to make lard. I was quick at that" to "Even if Tony had an affair, if it was a quickie affair, I'm sure we'd still be together. If it was a long one, I'm sure we'd get a divorce."

The inner life of the city—voices, children, baths, meals—has not undergone any substantial change since Jericho, the oldest city still inhabited. When Odysseus was finally united with Penelope, they talked all night in a cozy bed, under sheepskin covers. Children and the old are the same the world over. Only public lives are different: the automobile and airplane have made us nomads again. The city seems to be obsolete; a sense of community evaporates in all this mobility and stir. As persuasion is impotent in so distracted a world, and as our legislators seem to be mere pawns of lobbies, their hands hourly open to bribes, we must stoically wait out whatever awful hiatus there is to be between the technological destruction of the only known unit of civilization, the city, and its logical and natural reinvention, however that is to come about. Meanwhile, as a voice says in Zukofsky's *"A"-18*,

> . . .all
> their world's done to change the world is
> to make it more ugly to the airport.

Imaginary Americas

Of Sir Walter Scott's ornamental waterfall in the gardens at Abbotsford the Earl of Rokeby remarked that he could make a more respectable one from his own person. Peter Conrad, the English literary scholar, setting out to study versions of America (by which he means the United States) invented by various Englishmen who came here to find Utopia, themselves, the confirmation of their worst suspicions, Paradise, or the spearhead of technological advance, begins his analysis, as a warm-up for more thorough demonstrations, with a round of views of Niagara Falls from the sniff of Mrs. Trollope in 1827 to Bertrand Russell's blank stare in 1914.[1]

That sensibilities are predisposed to see what they want to see is the almost too predictable formula for precipitating the details of this lively book. Lively it is, as America is big and the English are accomplished observers and exiles with a purpose. There is nothing here of those travellers wholly unprepared for surprises. No Feisal of Arabia who, seeing his first waterfall (in Switzerland) asked politely of his companion Colonel Lawrence if they could remain until all the water had run over, no Sarmiento in Ohio in ecstasy at the towns and farms and well-behaved people, no Jardiel Poncela utterly appalled by California in the 1930s, no Marianne North having the time of her life (a sophisticated Alice in a real Wonderland) with Longfellow in Cambridge and General Grant in the White House, wondering in old age if both weren't a madcap dream.

The British have habitually chosen foreign places as scope for one crotchet or another (Arthur C. Clarke in Sri Lanka, Norman Douglas in Capri, An-

[1]Peter Conrad, *Imagining America* (New York: Oxford University Press, 1980).

thony Burgess in Malta). Peter Conrad is at his best with exiles like Auden, Huxley, and Isherwood whose visions of America scarcely correspond to anything at all, and who, with consummate eccentricity, made up Americas and lived quite imaginatively in them.

Conrad's approach to all of this is one of bright seriousness, an intellectual probing, a vigorous curiosity constantly turning up new information. His subject, helplessly, is so much the raw material of comedy that the glints of satire we perceive on every page shine alternately from Conrad's wit and from a ridiculousness innate in the careers being scrutinized. The psychedelic Huxley, a filthy Auden dabbled with snot and more than half-mad with buggery in his second childhood, Isherwood living in the upper reaches of the higher Hindu consciousness, Lawrence dithering about the phallic sunshine in New Mexico—they are a Thomas Love Peacock novel come true, a satire by Waugh, a set of Beerbohm cartoons, or Wyndham Lewis at his most outrageous.

It is all, however, quite real. These caricatures—men of genius, all—are exemplary experiments, a kind of pioneering in the spiritual dimension. In one sense, Conrad is analyzing America's reputation abroad by finding its sources in intelligent makers of opinion. Think of the many who know America from Céline's account of Detroit and Chicago, of those who trust Wells to know what he was talking about, of the goodwill between England and America created by Kipling. These articulate reports, however distorted, have an authority over rumor and clichés.

Jessie Whitehead, the daughter of Alfred North and friend of Gertrude Stein, once noted when she had lived half her life in England and half, until then, in the United States, that she preferred Americans because of their unfailing kindness. "What a boor Dr. Johnson would be at an American cocktail party." This is a clue to Conrad's choice of Englishmen in America: they were all outsiders in their own country, men of self-invention. They came here for the same reason that brought the Puritans, the Huguenots, the Anabaptists, and the Hassidim. Freedom from constraint and sanctions was not the only reason; Conrad is far more interested in the supposed America that fetched over his exiles, and in men in quest of something Europe lacked. Lawrence made up his America ludicrously out of the whole cloth of his lurid imagination.

Kipling was looking for a country in its epic stage of development, and proceeded to see America that way. *Captains Courageous* is a transparent hymn to derring-do, to sea captains on the Grand Banks and captains of industry. If America is also (in imitation of Europe) effete, we have heroic models to set us right. His novel discovers two heritages for an adolescent boy, one decadent (and significantly requiring a voyage to Europe), the other epic. Kipling tosses his protagonist off the depraved ocean liner taking him away from America, and has him rescued, reeducated, and remade by rough, manly fishermen.

Conrad spends a lot of energy studying *Captains Courageous*, and in his method inadvertently exposes the way he cuts corners and commits the very sin of his subjects in gazing with such raptness that he fools himself as to what he sees. He is particularly interested to take apart and inspect the scene in *Captains Courageous* where the tycoon Cheyne receives word in San Diego that his son Harvey is not after all dead, but has been picked up by a fishing boat and is safe in Gloucester. In his paraphrase, Conrad transfers to Cheyne actions belonging to his typist and telegrapher, as well as all the Chinese junks in San Diego harbor. Conrad rehearses the fine passage about Harvey's parents' transcontinental train journey, noting how Kipling is obsessed by facts and figures. (In America, by the way, we do not write $3,665.25 as $3,665\frac{1}{4}$, and in any case it should be, as in Kipling's text, $3,676.25.) Of Kipling's "The six-foot drivers were hammering their way to San Bernardino and the Mohave wastes . . ." Conrad says, "The narrative is so intent on numerical precision that Kipling even calculates the height of the engine driver (which is six feet), as if that were part of the equation." The "six-foot drivers" in question are the locomotive's shafts, which impart linear motion from steam-pushed pistons to the rotary motion of the wheels. Conrad's received opinion of Kipling as a perhaps pathological worshipper of tall and masculine men (for which Wells and Beerbohm berated him) blinds him to the text he is reading for us, and converts machinery into an *idée reçue*.

Conrad, in fact, has to be watched when he summarizes. Kipling's "almost bait up a trawl" (Harvey recounting his skills as a fisherman) becomes in Conrad "bait up a trawl." That "the representatives of $63 million worth of railroad interests cooperate in" Cheyne's record crossing of the continent is a sloppy way of combining two things: that the pertinent railroads involved were cooperative, and the worth of all American railroads. And so on. Conrad is apt to be wide-eyed in his reporting, and careless of details.

For all its historical sweep and tracking of changing English views of America, Conrad's study will stick in most readers' minds, I suspect, for its full-length portrait of Auden. He gives as much attention to Huxley and Isherwood, but their adventures are odd and atypical. Huxley the satirist ended by glorying in what he had once knocked, and Isherwood, who once sought an environment congenial to his nature in the Third Reich, found it in the California of Gerald Heard, bronzed lifeguards with a vocabulary of up to sixty words, and Swami Ramakrishna (who instructed him how to achieve "the ocean of perfection"). I once, to be polite to a lady, heard Gerald Heard lecture in St. Louis. He looked very El Greco, and spoke in long, suavely delivered sentences rich in names like Alyosha Karamazov, Epictetus, and St. Gregory of Nyssa, and in facts about the salinity of blood and seawater, evolution, and probably the transmigration of souls. Only in some high-toned Methodist preachers have I ever heard such beautiful rhetoric wrap itself around absolutely nothing.

Auden, however, belonged to this world, was an accomplished poet, was conversant with our culture in a way very few people are, and returned with irony and anguish to the Church of England. He came to America, or rather to New York, to be lonely. I think he came to insure that he was among humanity at its worst in this century. He could have gone to more terrible places, Rome for instance, but he wanted a place he could not romanticize. He recognized New York for what it is culturally, a trade center, a crossroads where everybody turns up sooner or later. It is also a city as European as it is American. It is our Alexandria, our Byzantium.

Here Auden fulfilled a desire (Conrad calls it a childish desire) to be of things while being apart from them, to live in his nursery of an apartment (by all accounts an incredibly nasty fox's den), outside of which (in bedroom slippers and unclean clothes) he delighted to play the spoiled brat to see, like an impossible child, how much he could get away with. He got away with everything, of course, as he was Auden. He became a monster of paradox, a social bully, an arrogant Christian, a foulmouthed old man with one of the most ravaged faces in history. The more awkward to be around he became, the more people sought him out, pleaded with him to speak, and valued his acquaintance.

He would, let us guess, have been quite a different Auden if he had remained in England. He annoyed the hell out of Oxford when he returned there to die. (He didn't die there, but in a hotel room in Austria, where he was buried to the strains of Wagner, as if he were an adjunct to Teutonic culture.) Auden and Isherwood, Conrad tells us, came to America together. Their paths diverged, both in search of liberty, "romantic privacies," to nurture their alienation. Conrad gives a brilliant analysis of the distance that developed between the two: Isherwood's love of health, cleanliness, and the sun; Auden's contrasting plunge into senility, dirt, and darkness—California and the "lawless marches" of New York City streets.

We begin to wonder as we follow Conrad's splendidly readable text what all this has to do with America. Is it not simply that stock device of novelists, the boardinghouse or ship or island where it is convenient to corral one's cast of characters? Conrad admits that America is so large and diverse that it will accommodate any questing soul who cares to arrive. It is still both a wilderness and a system of megalopolises, a backward and an advanced country, a mixture of its own and practically all other cultures.

America from the beginning was a promise of renewal for every human endeavor. It was an activity of the Renaissance, whose scholars and merchant princes effected its discovery and its first exploitation. Thereafter it exhibited an innocence (and concomitant ignorance) unavailable to Europe. Compare the American and French revolutions, Washington and Napoleon. What is pristine and a bit colorless in America is experienced and vastly more colorful in Europe. Looked at the other way around, what is weary and worn in Europe is spanking new in America.

Though we are now the oldest continuous government on the planet (with the possible exception of England, if you want to argue the point), we must still play the part of a recent arrival in politics and culture. Hence our appearance in the imagination of Wells and Kipling as a clean-hearted young giant from whom energy and hope can flow to the rest of the world.

Why did Ralph Hodgson and Ford Madox Ford end their days in Ohio? Aleksandr Kerenski spent the large part of his life here. There are immigrants and immigrants, and we tend to think of them as donations to our culture, shooed to Liberty's feet by the tyrannies of other lands. Thus we got Stravinsky, Audubon, Lipschitz, Ernst, Steinmetz, Fermi. Conrad is interested in quite a different kind of immigrant, one who has come uncompelled and had other choices. The purest example of this type is Heinrich Schliemann, who became an American citizen for the sheer panache of it.

The country is rich in such people, drawn here for reasons which we cannot appreciate (such as Jessie Whitehead's preferring American manners). The real lesson for us in Peter Conrad's study may be precisely to see qualities we are blind to, or take for granted.

There is nothing in this book, for instance, that fetched over Conrad's Englishmen which would tempt me to leave my backyard. It would be a cruel and unjust punishment were I obliged to live in Taos, Los Angeles, or New York City. I have, without actually going there, seen Niagara Falls.

Spiritual transplanting is not easy; strange things (as Conrad shows) happen to uprooted people. America didn't work for Kipling, or Hearn, or Mann, or Brecht. Napoleon, when the British nabbed him, was on his way to become an independent American farmer. I like to imagine him as having made it, as mayor of Cincinnati. Someone should study the psychology of coming to America. Conrad has pointed the way and set the example. Would Capone have been a somebody in Sicily? Would Hitchcock have made *Psycho* in England? Would Auden have shouted to guests in his bathroom not to use more than two sheets of toilet paper?